TABLE OF CONTENTS

INTRODUCTION.............................. 1

CHAPTER 1- I WAS ONLY A CHILD

CHAPTER 2- THE TRAGIC TRUTH

CHAPTER 3- DEEP SECRETS

CHAPTER 4- MY HOMETOWN

CHAPTER 5- THE RECOVERY

CHAPTER 6- LOVE CONQUERS ALL

CHAPTER 7- JUSTICE FOR ALL

CHAPTER 8- PRAYERS BEEN ANSWERED

CHAPTER 9- THE FINAL JUDGMENT

THE LORD IS MY SHEPHERD, I SHALL NOT WANT HE MAKETH ME TO LIE DOWN IN GREEN PASTURES HE LEADETH ME BESIDE THE STILL WATERS. HE RESTORETH MY SOUL HE LEADETH ME IN THE PATHS OF RIGHTEOUSESS FOR HIS NAME'S SAKE. YEA THOUGH I WALK THROUGH THE VALLEY OF THE SHADOW OF DEATH, I WILL FEAR NO EVIL FOR THOU ARE WITH ME, THEY ROD AND THY STAFF THEY COMFORT ME THOU PREPAREST A TABLE BEFORE ME IN THE PRESENCE OF MINE ENEMIES THOU ANOINTEST MY HEAD WITH OIL, AND MY CUP RUNNETH OVER. SURELY GOODNESS AND MERCY SHALL FOLLOW ME ALL THE DAYS OF MY LIFE, AND I WILL DWELL IN THE HOUSE OF THE LORD FOR EVER

THIS BOOK WAS WRITTEN AND CREATED BY RANDY FLORES AND IS FICTIONAL BASED ON TRUE LIFE EVENTS. THE LIFE OF RANDY AND ANDREA, WE COME FROM A SMALL TOWN SOUTH OF HOUSTON TEXAS. WHICH IS NAMED ROSENBERG TEXAS, WE BOTH HAD DIFFERENT LIFE'S MY PARENTS WERE WONDERFUL PARENTS FULL OF LOVE AND HAPPINESS ON THE OTHER HAND HERE PARENTS WERE MEAN TO HER. IN THIS STORY I HAVE THE OPPORTUNITY TO SHARE THE TRUE EVENTS, NAMES HAVE BEEN CHANGED TO PROTECT THE ACTUAL PERSON THESE THINGS GO ON EVERYDAY IN PEOPLE LIVES. BUT NO ONE SPEAKS UP BECAUSE THEY ARE SCARED TO DO SO OR TO EMBARRASSED, TO TAKE ACTION BUT I THANK GOD THAT AFTER ALL WE HAD BEEN THREW, WE NEVER LOST HOPE. OR GAVE UP I WANT TO THANK MY PARENTS FOR ALL THEY HAVE DONE FOR ME, AND I THANK JESUS CHRIST FOR GIVING ME THE KNOWLEDGE TO PUT THIS DOWN ON PAPER, WITHOUT OUR LORD AND SAVIOR WE ARE NOTHING.

CHAPTER 1   I WAS ONLY A CHILD

   I WAS BORN IN A SMALL TOWN SOUTH OF HOUSTON TEXAS CALLED ROSENBERG TEXAS; I WAS BROUGHT UP IN A GOOD HOME WITH GOOD STANDARDS WITH LOT'S OF LOVE. OUR PARENTS RASIED US WITH THE BEST OF THERE ABILITY, ALWAYS PROVIDED AND SHOW LOT'S OF LOVE AND COMPASSION. NOW ME AND MY 4 OLDER SIBLINGS WENT TO MY AUNT'S HOUSE, I WAS ONLY 7 YEARS OLD, WHICH THAT DAY WAS THE MOST TRAGIC DAY OF MY LIFE. I RECALL WE WERE GETTING READY TO GO TO MY AUNT'S HOUSE, AND FROM THERE WE WERE GOING TO THE PARK AS WE WOULD DO EVERY WEEKEND, BUT THIS WEEKEND CHANGE EVERYONE'S LIFE FOREVERY. I REMEMBER I WAS PLAYING WITH MY COUSIN'S AND HAVING A GOOD TIME WITH THEM, MY MOM AND AUNT WERE IN THE HOUSE GETTING FOOD READY FOR US. I WAS OUTSIDE PLAYING AROUND THE CARS, AND I HEARD THE SOUND I WILL NEVER FORGET, THE TRUCK HAD TURNED. ON I TRIED TO RUSH FORM UNDER

THE TRUCK I WAS HALFWAY OUT, AND THE TRUCK RAN OVER MY BACK BUSTED MY STOMACH WIDE OPEN. I GOT OUT FROM UNDER THE TRUCK HOLDING MY GUT'S IN MY HAND, THEN I FAIL TO THE GROUND, MY MOM AND AUNT CAME OUT THE HOUSE WITH TEARS IN THEIR EYES. THEY PICK ME UP AND RUSH ME TO THE HOSPITAL, I PASSED OUT ON OUR WAY TO THE HOSPITAL. MY AUNT STARTED GIVING ME CPR, TO START THE PROCESS OF SAVING MY LIFE, HALFWAY TO THE HOSPITAL THE CAR GOT A FLAT TIRE. MY MOM GOT OUT OF THE CAR IN TEAR'S FLAGGING OTHER CARS DOWN, FINALLY A CAR STOP WHICH TURN OUT TO BE A TAXI HE RUSHED US TO THE HOSPITAL, I REMEMBER ON MY WAY TO THE HOSPITAL I SAW MY MOM WITH THE SADDEST LOOK IN HER EYES. WHEN WE GOT TO THE HOSPITAL, THEY RUSHED ME TO THE OPERATING ROOM AND AS I WAS ON THE OPERATING TABLE MY MOM RUSHED TO LOOK FOR A PHONE. SHE WAS RUNNING UP AND DOWN THE HALL LOOKING FOR A PHONE, SHE CALLED MY DAD AT HIS JOB AS SOON AS MY DAD GOT THE NEWS THAT I HAD GOTTEN RAN OVER. HE DROPPED THE PHONE AND RUSHED TO THE HOSPITAL, AS HE SAW ME ON THE OPERATING TABLE FULL OF BLOOD, HE DROPPED TO HIS KNEES AND CRIED AND PRAYED FOR JESUS CHRIST TO SAVE ME. FROM THIS TERRIBLE ACCIDENT THAT I WAS IN, THIS ACCIDENT CAUSED MANY PEOPLE LOT'S OF PAIN AND SUFFERING, AS MY PARENT'S WERE EXPERIENCING WHAT WAS GOING ON THE DR. OPERATING ON ME COULD NOT DO ANYTHING FOR ME, MY STOMACH WAS BUSTED WIDE OPEN I LOST HALF A LIVER WHICH IT WAS FILLED WITH TINY ROCK'S. THE DR. TRIED AND TRIED TO HELP ME, BUT COULD NOT DO NOTHING FOR ME. AFTER ALL THESE HOURS OF THE DR. WORKING ON ME, THE SURGEON IN CHARGE HAD ME PUT ON AN EMERGENCY LIFE FLIGHT. I WAS TAKENT TO THE HOUSTON CHILDRENS HOSPITAL, THREW THE WHOLE TIME I DID NOT FEEL ANY PAIN, MY BODY WAS STILL IN SHOCK FROM ALL THAT HAPPEN. WHEN I GOT TO THE HOSPITAL, THEY RUSH ME INTO THE OPERATING ROOM AND AS THEY WERE OPERATIONG ON ME, I HAD DIED FOR 1 HOUR. AND WHEN I DIED, I SAW MY SOUL GOING TO HEAVEN, HALFWAY THERE AN ANGEL CAME DOWN PUT HIS HANDS ON MY SHOULDER'S AND PUSH MY SPIRIT BACK INTO MY BODY. BEFORE MY SPIRIT WENT BACK INTO MY BODY THE LORD SPOKE TO ME. AND SAID I AM NOT DONE WITH YOU YET, AS SOON AS HE SAID THIS, I WAS WAKING BACK UP AS I DID, I SAW THE DR. OVER ME NEVER GIVNG UP ON ME. I REMEMBER THAT DAY AS IF IT HAD JUST HAPPENED, A FEW DAYS AGO, I WOULD NEVER FORGET THAT DAY. I LOST 23 PINT'S OF BLOOD THERE WAS AN EMERGENCY BROADCAST THAT I NEEDED BLOOD DONATIONS, PEOPLE FROM ALL OVER CAME TO MY RESCUE, I STAYED IN THE HOSPITAL FOR THE TIME OF 6 WEEK'S. WHICH WAS AN EXPERIANCE TO

REMEMBER, LOT'S OF PEOPLE CAME TO VISIT ME AND BROUGHT ME LOT'S OF GIFTS AND GAVE ME LOT'S OF LOVE AND ATTENTION. I FELT THE LOVED BUT MOST OF ALL OUT OF ALL THAT WAS GOING ON, I NEW GOD'S PRESENCE WAS IN MY LIFE FOR IF IT WAS NOT BY HIS TENDER HANDS, LOVE AND MERCY I WOULD NOT HAVE SURVIVE THE ACCIDENT. AFTER 6 WEEKS IN THE HOSPITAL, I WAS FINALLY RELEASED ABLE TO GO HOME, THE WEEKS THAT FOLLOW WERE GOING TO BE A CHALLENGE, BEING ABLE TO WALK AND STAND AGAIN, AND BEING ABLE TO EAT AND HOLD MY FOOD DOWN. WITHOUT BRINGING PAIN TO MY STOMACH, WHICH WAS A HARD MISSION CAUSE EVERYTHING I DID OR ATE CAUSED PAIN, IT WAS GOING TO TAKE TIME TO RECOVER FROM MY ACCIDENT, BUT AS TIME WENT ON I WAS ABLE TO DEAL WITH MY INJURY AND DO WHAT I NEEDED TO DO TO GET OVER THIS SITUATION AND MOVE ON WITH MY LIFE. IT IS GETTING CLOSE TO BE MY BIRTHDAY I WILL BE TURNING 8 YEARS OLD, MY MOM AND DAD HAD PLANNED A SURPRISE PARTY FOR ME, AND IT SURELY WAS A SURPRISING DAY. ALL OF MY FRIENDS AND FAMILY WERE ALL THERE AT THE PARK WAITING FOR ME TO SHOW UP, AS I SAW EVERYONE THEIR TEARS FAIL FROM MY EYES. MY MOM ASKED ME WHAT WAS WRONG AND I STAYED SILENT, THEN I SAID NOTHING MOM EVERYTHING IS GREAT I NEVER NEW SO MANY PEOPLE LOVED ME AND CARE FOR ME. SO IT WAS A GREAT DAY I RECIVED LOT'S OF GIFTS, AS A CHILD I EXPERIENCED A LOT OF DIFFERENT SITUATIONS, SOME GOOD AND SOME BAD BUT OVERALL, MY LIFE AS A CHILD WAS EVERYTHNGS I WANTED IT TO BE. I WAS SLOWLY GETTING OVER MY DEADLY ACCIDENT AND I STILL HAVE FLASHBACKS FROM THAT DAY, I FEEL THAT NO MATTER HOW MANY YEARS PASS I'LL NEVER FORGET THAT TRAGIC OF THAT DAY. WILL JUST A FEW MORE DAY'S AND SUMMER IS OVER AND IT WILL BE TIME TO GO BACK TO SCHOOL, THE FIRST DAY OF SCHOOL WAS NOT SO GREAT, THERE WERE STILL LOT'S OF THINGS GOING ON IN MY LIFE. THAT I DID NOT KNOW IF I WAS READY TO START SCHOOL SO SOON AFTER ALL THAT HAS HAPPEN IN THE SUMMER. 1ST PERIOD WAS GYM I WAS EMBARRASSED TO TAKE OFF MY SHIRT, I DID NOT WANT PEOPLE TO BE STARING AT ME OR MAKE FUNNY REMARKS ABOUT MY SCARE ON MY STOMACH. THE WHOLE TIME WHEN I WAS IN SCHOOL, I KEPT TO MYSELF, I WAS CAUGHT UP IN MY PRIVATE WORLD STRUGGLING WITH MY SITUATION WONDERING WHAT WOULD BECOME OF MY LIFE. I WAS STILL AT A YOUNG AGE BUT AFTER THE ACCIDENT MY WHOLE LIFE CHANGED, I LOOKED AT THINGS AT A DIFFERENT WAY THAN OTHER PEOPLE, FOR THE FIRST 2 MONTHS I KEPT TO MYSELF WANTING TO HAVE NO CONTACT WITH ANYONE. WITH THE SCARY THOUGHT OF SOMEONE ASKING OF MY ACCIDENT, IT WAS AN UNPLEASANT EXPERIENCE EATING LINCH BY MYSELF KEEPING TO MYSELF, AT THE

PLAYGROUND I WOULD JUST SIT THEIR SILENT, SO MY FIRST YEAR BACK WAS AN UNPLEASANT EXPERIENCE. NOT BECAUSE THE OTHER KIDS TREATED ME BAD, EVERYONE WAS TRYING TO BE MY FRIEND, BUT THE INSECURITY OF MY SELF KEPT ME FROM TALKING TO ANYONE AND NOT MAKING FRIENDS. THEN ONE DAY DURING LUNCH I WAS EATING BY MYSELF, AND THIS BOY IN MY CLASS CAME UP TO ME AND SPOKE TO ME, HELLO I'M TIM, I NOTICE YOU HAVE BEEN KEEPING TO YOUR SELF ALL THIS TIME DO YOU MIND IF I SIT AND EAT MY LUNCH WITH YOU? I HESITATED FOR A BIT THEN I SAID THAT'S FINE, YOU CAN SIT HERE MY NAME IS RANDY HOW ARE YOU DOING? I AM OK I WAS JUST WONDERING HOW ARE YOU DOING I'VE SEEN HAVE BEEN BY YOURSELF ALMOST THE WHOLE SCHOOL YEAR, MAY I ASK WHY, WILL IT'S EMBARRASSING TO SAY, BUT LAST SUMMER I WAS IN A TERRIBLE CAR ACCIDENT I ALMOST DIED, AND IT LEFT AN UGLY SCARE ON MY STOMACH, SO I GUESS I AM JUST EMBARRASSED THAT PEOPLE MAY FIND OUT AND MAKE FUN OF ME, NO RANDY YOU ARE SO WRONG NO ONE WILL MAKE FUN OF YOU WE HAVE BEEN TRYING TO TALK TO YOU WE WANT TO BE YOUR FRIEND. BUT YOU NEVER GAVE ANYONE THE CHANCE TO TALK TO YOU I KNOW TIM, I WAS JUST INSECURE ABOUT HOW I LOOK WILL I MEAN HOW MY STOMACH LOOKS, IT IS OK RANDY NOW YOU KNOW WE ARE ALL YOUR FRIENDS NO ONE IS HERE TO HURT YOU. WE ARE HERE TO MAKE SURE YOU ARE HAPPY. THANK YOU, TIM, FOR MAKING ME FEEL BETTER ABOUT MYSELF, AND TO KNOW THAT I HAVE PEOPLE THAT CARE ABOUT MY HAPPINESS, WE FOUND OUR SELVES JUST TALKING AND TALKING. HE BECAME MY BEST FRIEND. AFTER THAT DAY, MY LIFE STARTED TO CHANGE, I FOUND MYSELF NOT BEING SO INSECURE AND THE REST OF THE SCHOOL YEAR TURNED OUT GREAT, THAT DAY WAS A CHANGING LIFE AND A NEW EXPERIENCE THANKS TO THAT ONE PERSON. THAT TOOK TIME OUT OF HIS LIFE TO MAKE MY LIFE A BETTER ONE, I LOOK FORWARD TO THE REST OF THE SCHOOL YEAR. THE NEXT DAY I WAS IN THE PLAYGROUND WITH MY FRIEND TIM, WE SAT AND TALKED THEN ONE BY ONE OTHER BOY'S AND GIRL'S CAME UP TO ME, AND STARTED TALKING TO ME FROM THAT POINT I FELT AS IF I HAD A PLACE IN LIFE AND A PLACE IN THAT SCHOOL, AND THEN I STARTED GETTING INVITED TO BIRTHDAY PARTIES AND SLEEPOVERS. BY THE END OF THE SCHOOL YEAR, I HAD MORE FRIENDS THAN I COULD HAVE IMAGINED, AND THIS HOLD TIME I WAS WORRIED OF WHAT PEOPLE WOULD THINK OF ME. WHEN THIS WHOLE TIME THEIR ONLY THOUGHT WAS WHEN WOULD I COME AROUND AND OPEN UP TO THEM, AND NO ONE ASK ME ABUT MY SCARS OR ACCIDENT, IT WAS JUST MY INSECURITY THAT KEPT ME DOWN THE SCHOOL YEAR IS ALMOST OVER ONLY A FEW MORE WEEKS IT WILL BE SUMMER TIME. I PRAY THIS SUMMER WILL BE BETTER THAN LAST SUMMER

WHICH WILL ALWAYS BE THE SUMMER OF MY LIFE, THAT I STORE IN THE BACK OF MY MIND A REMINDER OF HOW BLESSED I AM TO BE ALIVE, AND ABLE TO ENJOY THE LOVE AND HAPPINESS OF MY FAMILY AND FRIENDS. TODAY I AM GOING BACK TO MY AUNT'S HOUSE THE PLACE WHERE MY ACCIDENT HAPPEN, I HAVE NOT BEEN BACK TO HER HOUSE SINCE THAT DAY SO I WILL SEE HOW I FEEL THE THOUGHT OF GOING BACK THEIR TO WHERE MY TRAGEDY HAPPEN. IT IS GOING TO BE A INTERESTING DAY, I AM KINDA OF NERVOUS TO GO BUT IT IS SOMETHING THAT MUST BE DONE SO I CAN GET OVER THIS CHAPTER IN MY LIFE, AS I AM ON MY WAY TO MY AUNT'S HOUSE I START TO GET NERVOUS AS WE PULL UP TO HER HOUSE I STAY IN THE CAR FOR A BIT WITH TEARS IN MY EYES, THEN I SLOWLY GET OUT OF THE CAR AS I STAND I LOOK DOWN I CAN STILL SEE THE BLOOD SPOTS ON THE GROUND, THEN I SAW THAT RIGHT THERE WHERE I STAND WAS THE SPOT THAT I ALMOST LOST MY LIFE, I DROP TO MY KNEES AND STARTED CRYING LIKE A BABY. MY MOM CAME UP TO ME AND ASK ME IF EVERYTHING WAS OK I LOOKED AT HER WITH THE SADDEST EYES, AND SAID YES MOM I AM OK I WAS JUST THINKING ABOUT THAT DAY I ALMOST DIED , BUT GOD SAID IT WAS NOT MY TIME TO GO YES RANDY GOD SAVED YOU HE HAVE'S PLANS FOR YOU, AFTER A SLIGHT PAUSE I WAS ABLE TO ACCEPT THAT DAY, AND THEN I WENT TO MY AUNT A GAVE HER A BIG HUG AND SAID THANK YOU FOR BEING THERE FOR ME AND NEVER GAVE UP ON ME BECAUSE OF YOU I MADE IT. AND NOW I AM ABLE TO LIVE MY LIFE AS GOD HAS PLANNED IT TO BE, NOW AS I LOOK EVERYTHING IS FALLING INTO PLACE, I AM FINDING PEACE IN MY LIFE I HAVE GONE OVER HIGH HURDLES I HAVE BEEN THREW ALOT, BUT THREW IT ALL AND ALL I HAVE OVERCOME ALL THE OBSTACLES I HAVE FACED. NOW IT'S TIME FOR A NEW JOURNEY IT'S TIME TO LEAVE MY AUNT'S HOUSE AND GO ON WITH MY LIFE, TOMORROW WILL BE AN INTERESTING DAY I WILL BE ABLE TO TELL MY FRIENDS ABOUT MY VISIT, TO MY AUNT'S HOUSE AND WHAT I EXPERIENCED DURING MY VISIT AFTER SCHOOL TOMORROW I HAVE A DR. APPOINTMENT WITH A NEUROLOGIST. I HAVE BEEN EXPERIENCING DRUNK SPILLS AND SEE THINGS THAT ARE NOT THERE, I WOULD WAKE UP CRYING AND SCARED TO WALK CAUSE I WOULD SEE LOT'S AND LOT'S OF EYES ALL OVER THE FLOOR AND IN THE AIR, SO I PRAY THE DR. CAN HELP AND GIVE ME A RELIEVING ANSWER, I WAS TIRED OF WHAT I EXPERIENCED EVERY MORNING. AS RANDY FALLS ASLEEP ALL HE COULD THINK ABOUT WAS HIS VISIT TO HIS AUNT'S HOUSE, AND HOW THINGS WERE GOING TO BE THE FOLLOWING DAY WHICH WAS GOING TO BE A BIG DAY MORNING WILL BE HERE SOON LET'S SEE WHAT HAPPENS NEXT. GOOD MORNING TIM I HAVE SOME INTRESTING NEWS TO TELL YOU, WHAT IS IT RANDY TELL ME? WILL I WENT TO MY AUNT'S HOUSE YESTERDAY WHERE THE ACCIDENT

HAPPEND AND WHEN I GOT THERE I BUSTED OUT IN TEARS, BUT THEN I FELT A SINCE OF BEING RELIEVE OF EVERYTHING THAT HAPPEN THERE THAT DAY. THAT'S GREAT RANDY I AM SO GLAD TO HEAR THAT YOU ARE DOING MUCH BETTER, YES MY FRIEND I AM, THANK YOU I HAVE A DR. APPOINTMENT TODAY AFTER SCHOOL TO SEE HOW I AM DOING, DON'T WORRY RANDY YOU WILL BE OK WILL I HAVE TO GO TO THE DR. NOW I WILL LET YOU KNOW HOW IT GOES, AS RANDY GOES TO THE DR. OFFICE ALL HE CAN DO IS THINK ABOUT WHAT THE DR. WILL TELL HIM. HELLO DR. CRUZ PLEASE TELL ME WHY I AM FEELING LIKE THIS I AM TIRED OF THIS PLEASE HELP, OK RANDY LET ME EXAMINE YOU AND SEE WHAT IS GOING ON IN YOUR HEAD AFTER A LONG EXAMINATION. THE DR TOLD ME THAT I HAVE A LOT OF ELECTRICITY IN MY BRAIN DUE TO THE ACCIDENT, AND IT WILL RESOLVE IN THE YEARS TO COME IT TOOK ME YEARS AFTER THE ACCIDENT TO OVERCOME, IT'S MORNING TIME TO GO TO SCHOOL AS I GET TO SCHOOL, I SAW MY BEST FRIEND AND HE TOLD ME THAT HE HAD SOMETHING VERY IMPORTANT TO TELL ME LATER HE LOOKED AT ME WITH A SAD LOOK AND TEARS IN HIS EYES. HE TOLD ME THE MOST HEART BREAKING NEWS HIS DAD HAD GOT ANOTHER JOB IN A DIFFERENT STATE, SO THIS WILL BE HIS LAST YEAR IN SCHOOL HERE, MY HEART DROPPED HE WAS MORE THAN JUST A FRIEND HE WAS LIKE A BROTHER. BUT RANDY I WILL ALWAYS BE HERE FOR YOU WHEN EVER YOU NEED ME JUST REACH OUT TO ME AND I WILL BE THERE FOR YOU, AND IF YOU EVER FEEL LOST LOOK UP INTO THE SKY AND THERE YOU WILL FIND THE ANSWERE, THAT WILL SET YOU FREE AT FIRST I DID NOT UNDERSTAND WHAT HE WAS SAYING THEN THE DAY CAME AND I FELT ALONE, I REMEMBER WHAT TIM HAD TOLD ME TO DO SO I LOOKED UP INTO THE SKY AND THEN I SAW MY HAPPINESS, AT THAT POINT I NEW ALL I HAD TO DO WAS ASK GOD TO SET ME FREE FROM THIS AND I KNOW THIS IS TIM LAST YEAR OF SCHOOL WITH ME, BUT I WILL NEVER FORGET HIM FOR HE HAS SHOW HIS LOVE FOR ME AS A FRIEND AND A BROTHER.

CHAPTER 2   THE TRAGIC TRUTH

MY PARENTS WERE ALWAYS THERE FOR ME THEY ALWAYS SHOWED ME THAT LOVE OF A PARENT AS IT SHOULD BE, AS I THINK ABOUT EVERYTHING, I AM FOREVER BLESSED TO HAVE SUCH WONDERFUL PARENTS. AND I AM ALSO VERY NERVOUS ABOUT MY FIRST DAY BACK IN SCHOOL, NEXT YEAR I DO NOT KNOW HOW I AM GOING TO SURVIVE WITHOUT MY BEST FRIEND TIM, HE WAS ALWAYS THERE FOR ME AND SHOWED ME THAT I COULD MAKE IT NO MATTER WHAT HAPPENS IN LIFE. THE TIME IS NEAR FOR THE SCHOOL YEAR TO START, THIS SUMMER WENT BY SO QUICK IT FEELS LIKE A DREAM THAT I DID NOT EXPECT TO END SO SOON, I FINALLY MADE IT TO THE 8TH GRADE BUT I DON'T KNOW IF I AM READY TO FACE MY NEW YEAR WITHOUT TIM BY MY SIDE, AND TO MEET NEW PEOPLE THAT I NEVER SEEN BEFORE I FEEL LIKE THE 5TH GRADE IS STARTING ALL OVER AGAIN, I WILL BE ALL ALONE NO ONE TO TALK TO THERE WILL NEVER BE A FRIEND LIKE MY BROTHER. WILL I AM GOING TO SLEEP AND BE READY TO FACE WHAT TOMORROW HAS TO OFFER, AS RANDY SLEEPS HE CRYS IN HIS SLEEP HE IS SCARED TO FACE THE WORLD, WITHOUT HIS FRIEND LITTLE DOES HE KNOWS WHAT WAITS FOR HIM AT SCHOOL LET'S SEE WHAT HAPPENS NEXT. WILL THE TIME HAS COME TO GO TO SCHOOL AT LEASE THIS TIME I DO NOT HAVE GYM 1ST PERIOD, BUT ONE THING THAT WILL ALWAYS KEEP ME STRONG AND KEEP ME GOING IS PUTTING GOD FIRST IN EVERYTHING I DO, AND I HAVE MY BEST FRIEND TO THANK FOR INTRODUCING ME TO OUR LORD AND SAVIOR, MOM ALWAYS TOLD ME SON IN LIFE ALWAYS EXPECT THE UNEXPECTED, FOR ONLY THEN YOU WILL SEE WHAT LIFE IS ALL ABOUT. MOM ALWAYS HAD A SPECIAL WAY OF PUTTING THINGS SO I COULD UNDERSTAND, WHAT SHE WAS TELLING ME I JUST FEEL SO INSECURE AND ALONE KNOWING I'M GOING TO START A NEW SCHOOL YEAR, ALL ALONE AS I ARRIVED TO SCHOOL, I SEE LOT'S OF NEW FACES I DID NOT SEE LAST YEAR, AND PEOPLE THAT I SPENT TIME WITH IN THE PASS SO THIS NEW START MIGHT NOT BE THAT BAD AFTER ALL. I JUST HAVE TO MOVE FORWARD AND LEAVE THE PASS IN THE PASS AND CONTINUE MY LIFE AS

GOD HAS INTENDED ME TO DO, AS I GET OUT OF THE CAR, I START WALKNG TOWARDS THE OFFICE TO GET MY CLASSROOM SCHEDULE AS I APPROACH THE OFFICE I HEAR A FAMILIAR VOICE. AS I TURN AND LOOK IT IS TIM'S OTHER BEST FRIEND MARK WHO STARTED TO BE A GOOD FRIEND TO ME ALSO, IT WAS A RELIFE TO SEE HIM, HEY MARK HOW ARE YOU DOING GOOD TO SEE YOU I AM GOOD HOW ARE YOU DOING RANDY, WILL HONESTLY I WAS KINDA SCARE I DID NOT KNOW WHAT TO EXPECT. BUT I NEW THINGS WERE GOING TO TURN OUT GREAT AND NOW THAT I KNOW YOU ARE HERE, EVERYTHING WILL BE GOOD YES RANDY JUST TAKE IT ONE DAY AT A TIME, AND YOU WILL BE JUST FINE. YOUR RIGHT MARK BUT I AM STILL A LITTLE NERVOUS ABOUT MY NEW SCHOOL YEAR HE LOOKED AT ME AND PUT HIS HAND ON MY SHOULDER AND SAID TO ME MY FRIEND YOU HAVE NOTHING TO FEAR. I AM HERE BY YOUR SIDE AND I WILL MAKE SURE THAT EVERYTHING WILL BE GREAT FOR YOU, SO PUT ALL FEARS AND DOUBTS OUT OF YOUR HEAD ADN ENJOY YOUR NEW SCHOOL YEAR, IT IS MUCH DIFFERENT THAN WHERE YOU COME FROM, I ASSURE YOU THAT HERE YOU WILL HAVE A NEW START IN YOUR LIFE AND CREATE NEW MEMORIES THAT YOU WILL ALWAYS REMEMBER AND USE IN YOUR LIFE. REMEMBER MY FRIEND IT IS NEVER TO LATE FOR A NEW START IN LIFE; AFTER HEARING THESE WORDS I WAS SET AT EASE THANKS MARK I NEEDED TO HEAR THAT NOW LET ME GO GET MY SCHEDULE I WILL TALK TO YOU LATER TODAY, AS I GET READY TO GO TO THE OFFICE I SEE THE MOST BEAUTIFUL VISION THE GIRL I USED TO GO TO SCHOOL WITH, I NEVER GOT A CHANCE TO TALK TO HER BECAUSE SHE HAD MOVED OUT OF TOWN BEFORE THE SCHOOL YEAR WAS OVER, AND NOW SHE IS BACK BECAUSE HER FAMILY HAD MOVED BACK SO NOW THAT SHE HAS RETURN I WILL DO MY BEST TO TALK TO HER, AND HOPEFULLY MAKE HER MY GIRLFRIEND I AM FINISHING UP IN THE OFFICE, AS I WALK OUT OF THE OFFICE WE GLANCE AT EACH OTHER I LOOKED AT HER AS SHE SMILED AND LOOKED INTO MY EYES, AS SHE WALKED INTO THE OFFICE I STAYED OUTSIDE IN A DAZE JUST LOOKING AT HER THROUGHT THE GLASS WINDOWN, WAITING FOR HER TO COME BACK OUT AND HOPEFULLY I WOULD WORK UP THE COURAGE TO TALK TO HER, AS I WOULD THINK OF WHAT I WOULD TELL HER AS IF I HAD PLANNED OUT WHAT I WOULD TELL HER AND NOW THE MOMENT HAS COME FOR ME TO MAKE MY MOVE AND TALK TO HER. BUT AS SHE CAME OUT AND LOOK AT ME, I FROZE AND WAS SILENT AS SHE CAME TO ME, SHE STOOD THERE WITHOUT SAYING A WORD AS IF SHE WAS TRYING TO REMEMBER WHO I WAS, AND FINALLY SHE SPOKE AND WHEN SHE SAID THE FIRST WORDS TO ME MY HEART DROPPED. SHE HAD THE MOST BEAUTIFUL VOICE A VOICE OF AN ANGEL SHE SAID IN A SOFT TONE HI YOUR RANDY RIGHT, AND I KINDA HESITATED FOR A MOMENT BEFORE I SPOKE

YES, I AM HOW DO YOU REMEMBER ME AND I THOUGHT YOU AND YOUR FAMILY MOVED OUT OF TOWN SO WHAT HAPPEND, AND HER RESPONSE WAS MY DAD'S JOB ENDED SO WE HAD NO CHOICE BUT TO MOVE BACK INTO TOWN. BUT AS SHE WAS TELLING ME THIS, I SAW IN HER EYES SHE WAS HIDING A DEEP SECREAT, BUT I SAID NOTHING ABOUT WHAT I WAS THINKING SO I RESPONDED TO HER, OH OK WILL THAT IS GREAT I AM GLAD YOU CAME BACK TO SCHOOL I WAS HOPING YOU WOULD COME BACK AND HERE YOU ARE IN FRONT OF ME, LOOKED ANDREA I HAVE SOMETHING I NEED TO TELL YOU, SHE LOOKED AT ME PUZZLED AND ASK WHAT IS IT I CLEARED MY THROAT AND SAID IN A LOW VOICE I HAVE AND BEEN HAVING AND STILL DO HAVE THE BIGGEST CRUSH ON YOU. BUT I ALWAYS WAS SCARED TO SAY ANYTHING BECAUSE I DID NOT WANT TO BE TURN DOWN THAT RIGHT THERE WOULD HAVE CRUSH ME, SO I STAYED SILENT AND NOT SAID A WORD THERE WERE MANY TIMES I JUST WANTED TO GO UP TO YOU GRAB YOUR HAND AND SAY ANDREA I LIKE YOU ALOT. AND I WANT US TO BE TOGETHER AND I TELL YOU LOT'S OF TIMES I CAME CLOSE TO DOING IT BUT EVERY TIME I SAW YOU, I FROZE AND NOW I AM SAYING IT ANDREA, I LIKE YOU ALOT I HAVE ALWAYS LIKE YOU AND I ALWAYS WILL AFTER I TOLD HER THIS SHE WAS SHOCKED AND STAYED SILENT, WHEN I SAW HER REACTION I SAID OK I SHOULD HAVE NOT SAID ANYTHING I WILL LET YOU GET TO CLASS AND LEAVE YOU ALONE, AS I WAS WALKING AWAY SHE SAID NO STOP WHAT IS IT THEN SHE SURPRISE ME WHEN SHE SAID TO ME YOU KNOW RANDY FOR MANY YEARS I COUGHT MYSELF THINKING ABOUT YOU. I NEVER NEW WHY MY THOUGHTS WERE ALWAYS ON YOU IF WE NEVER TALKED THEN I ASKED HER SO WHAT ARE YOU SAYING, I JUST PRAY YOU ARE TELLING ME WHAT I THINK YOU ARE SHE LOOKED INTO MY EYES AND SAID WHAT DO YOU THINK I AM SAYING, I AM TELLING YOU THAT I LIKE YOU MORE THAN YOU CAN IMAGINE THAT DAY MY LIFE LONG CRUSH FINALLY BECAME MY GIRLFRIEND, THAT DAY BECAME THE HAPPIEST DAY OF MY LIFE AT LEASE I THOUGHT IT WAS I DID NOT EXPECT WHAT THE NEAR FUTURE WOULD BRING THAT WILL CHANGED, EVERYTHING AND HOW I LOOK AT LIFE. WE WENT ON WITH OUR DAY IN SCHOOL I WAS SO HAPPY I INTRODUCHED HER TO ALL MY FRIENDS, AND THERE WAS NOTHING THAT I WOULD NOT DO FOR HER ALL SHE HAD TO DO WAS JUST ASK AND IT WOULD BE DONE. WE ARE IN THE LAST PERIOD AND I HAVE HER FOR MY LAST PERIOD THE WHOLE TIME IN CLASS WE DID NOT PAY ATTENTION TO THE TEACHER, WE WOULD JUST SEND EACH OTHER NOTES JUST GIGGLE AT EACH OTHER IT WAS THE TIME OF OUR LIVES, AFTER SCHOOL, SHE ASKED ME WHAT WAS I DOING? I AM NOT DOING NOTHING WHY YOU ASK I WOULD LIKE FOR YOU TO COME TO MY HOUSE I HAVE A FEW FRIENDS COMING OVER JUST TO HANG OUT, I WOULD

LIKE TO INTRODUCE YOU TO THEM SO I THOUGHT ABOUT IT AND SAID OK THAT WOULD BE GREAT I WILL GO OVER THERE IN A WHILE. I WILL MEET YOU AT YOUR HOUSE LATER, OK RANDY TRY NOT TO BE TO LONG OK I WON'T BE THAT LONG GREAT WE ARE GOING TO HAVE LOT'S OF FUN. AS SHE LEFT ALL KINDS OF THOUGHTS WERE GOING THREW MY HEAD WHAT KIND OF FUN IS SHE TALKING ABOUT WHAT ARE WE GOING TO DO, I HOPE IT IS NOTHING BAD OR ILLEGAL I AM JUST OVER THINKING THINGS, I KNOW ANDREA IS A GOOD PERSON SHE HAS NOT SHOWED ANYTHING OUT OF THE ORDINARY. AS I AM WALKING HOME, I SEE HER TALKING TO OTHER BOY'S AND GIRLS AS THEY ALL STAND THERE LAUGING AND ACTING NOT SO NORMAL. I STAND THERE FOR A MOMENT AND JUST LOOK AT THEM THEN I TURN AND WALK AWAY WITHOUT LOOKING BACK I GET HOME; I STARTED GETTING READY THEN I PAUSED FOR A MOMENT AND STARTED THINKING ABOUT WHAT SHE HAD TOLD ME ABOUT THE GET TOGETHER AT HER HOUSE AND I ALSO STARTED THINKING ABOUT OUR FIRST CONVERSATION, THAT WAS A DREAM COME TRUE, THEN I SAID TO MYSELF HOW CAN SOME ONE SO SWEET AND BEAUTIFUL DO ANYTHNG WRONG, WHAT WOULD CAUSE HURT AND PAIN TO HERSELF OR A LOVED ONE. AT THAT POINT I FELT THAT I HAD NOTING TO WORRY ABOUT. I PUT IT OUT OF MY HEAD AS IF THAT THOUGHT NEVER CROSS MY MIND AND STARTED GETTING READY TO GO OVER TO HER HOUSE, MY BEAUTIFUL GIRLFRIEND THEN AS I WAS LEAVING MY FRIEND CAME TO MY HOUSE, HE MARK WHAT ARE YOU DOING JUST CAME TO SEE HOW YOU DOING WHERE ARE YOU GOING, WHERE DO YOU THINK I AM GOING OVER TO MY GIRLFRIENDS HOUSE SHE HAS SOME OF HER FRIENDS GOING OVER SHE SAID WE GOING TO HANG OUT AND HAVE FUN, HE LOOKED AT ME AND STAYED SILENT MARK WHAT IS IT. LOOKED RANDY THERE IS SOMETHING I NEED TO TELL YOU ABOUT ANDREA, TELL ME WHAT IS IT HE PUT HIS HEAD DOWN AND THEN LOOKED AT ME WITH THE SADDEST LOOK I EVER SEEN. I AM GOING TO TELL YOU SOMETHING ABOUT ANDERA THAT I HAVE KNOWN FOR MANY YEARS, AND IT HAS BEEN A BIG SECRET IN MY LIFE AND I AM TIRED OF HOLDING THIS IN SO HERE IT GOES, SEE YOUR GIRLFRIEND ANDREA HAS HAD A BAD LIFE HER PARENTS WERE NOT SUCH GOOD PARENT'S, THEY HAD MANY PROBLEMS AND WOULD SOMETIMES TAKE IT OUT ON ANDREA THEY HAD GOT REPORTED TO THE AUTHORITY, AND WHEN THEY FOUND OUT THEY WERE GETTING IN TROUBLE WITH THE LAW'S THEY WOULD MOVE OUT OF TOWN, AND HERE WE GO A FEW YEARS LATER THEY ARE BACK, WITH TEARS IN MY EYES, MARK I NEED YOU TO TELL ME EVERYTHING RIGHT NOW WHAT HAPPEN TO HER AND HOW DO YOU KNOW ALL OF THIS. OK RANDY HERE GOES THE WHOLE STORY HE TAKES A DEEP BREATH, WITH TEARS IN HIS EYES I KNOW ALL OF THIS BECAUSE SHE USE TO BE

TOGETHER WITH MY FRIEND SAM. WHEN HE HEARD WHAT WAS HAPPENING TO HER HE LOST IT AND ENDED HIS LIFE, THAT REALLY DESTROYED ANDREA KNOWING ANOTHER PERSON KILLED THEM SELF CAUSE WHAT SHE WAS GOING THREW, OK NOW IT STARTED WHEN SHE HAD JUST 9 YRS OLD WAIT WHAT YOU MEAN 9 YRS OLD, OH MY GOD TELL ME SHE STAYED WITH HER MOM AND DAD AND LITTLE BROTHER, THINGS SEEMED TO BE GOOD ON OUTSIDE BUT ON THE INSIDE SHE EXPERIENCED TORTURE AND PAIN, IN THE MORNING SHE WOULD WAKE UP TO YELLING AND GETTING HIT WITH THE BELT OR WHATEVERY THEY COULD FIND. SHE WOULD COME TO SCHOOL WITH BLACK EYES AND BRUISES AND THEY WOULD TELL HER ALL KINDS OF BAD THINGS, LIKE YOUR UGLY YOU ARE NOT MY CHILD WHY DON'T YOU RUN AWAY OR KILL YOUR SELF DO US ALL A FAVOR. SO WHY DID'NT SHE LEAVE SHE STAYED BECAUSE SHE WAS WORRIED ABOUT HER LITTLE BROTHER SO HER MOM TOLD HER HURRY UP AND GET OUT OF THIS HOUSE, YOU ARE A WASTE OF SPACE THEN THEY WOULD SLAP HER AND THE OTHER KID THEY WOULD HUG AND SHOWED HIM LOVE AND HAPPINESS.THEN WHEN HER FATHER WOULD GET HOME FROM WORK, THE FIRST THING HE WOULD DO IS GO TO HER ROOM AND HE SPANKED HER AND SHE WOULD CRY AND BEG HIM TO STOP, BUT HE WOULD JUS LAUGH AND HIT HER HARDER BUT THE MOST TERRIBLE PART OF ALL OF THIS THEY WOULD DRINK ALOT AND RANDY WHEN HE SAID MY NAME HE PAUSED, WHAT IS IT MARK HE TOOK A DEEP BREATH AND SAID WHEN HER DAD WOULD GET DRUNK HE WOULD HAVE HIS WAY WITH HER, HE TOOK HER INNOCENCE WHAT NO MARK THAT IS NOT SO HOW CAN A DAD DO THAT TO HIS OWN DAUGHTER TELL ME MARK THIS DID NOT HAPPEN, NO MARK I CAN NOT BELIEVE THAT MY GOD HOW CAN THIS HAPPEN, RANDY THIS IS JUST THE START OF IT WHAT THERE IS MORE YES SO THAT WEEK THAT IT HAPPENED SHE WAS NOWHERE TO BE FOUND THE WHOLE WEEK WE LOOK FOR HER, BUT SHE WAS NOT THERE HER PARENTS SENT HER AWAY FOR THE WEEK TO GO STAY WITH A FAMILY MEMBER, AND DID SHE TELL HER MOM WHAT HER DAD DID TO HER THAT NIGHT YES SHE DID TELL HER MOM, AND WHAT DID HER MOM SAY SHE SLAPPED HER AND SAID STOP YOUR LYING YOU KNOW WHAT THE TRUTH IS, YOU LAY WITH A BOY AND NOW YOUR BLAMING YOUR DAD FOR WHAT YOU DID YOU KNOW IT'S NOT RIGHT, I CAN NOT STAND YOU I AM SENDING YOU AWAY FOR THE WEEK GO OVER TO MY SISTER'S HOUSE AND LET HER DEAL WITH YOUR LIE'S I'M DONE SO THEY SENT HER OFF FOR THE WEEK. WHEN SHE CAME BACK TO SCHOOL THE FOLLOWING WEEK, SHE WAS A TOTALLY DIFFERENT PERSON MARK WHAT DO YOU MEAN TELL ME WITH TEARS IN MY EYES I COULD BEARLY TAKE IT WHAT HE IS TELLING ME. SEE SHE USED TO BE ALIVE ENJOYING LIFE ADN VERY TALKATIVE, WITH EVERYONE IT

LOOKED LIKE EVERYTHING WAS GREAT SHE COVER HER PAIN VERY WELL, BUT THIS TIME YOU COULD SEE IT WAS IN HER FACE AND THE WAY SHE WAS ACTING SOMETHING WAS NOT RIGHT, WE WENT ON WITH THE DAY AND THROUGOUT THE DAY WE WERE CONFUSED. AND WONDERING WHAT HAPPENED TO HER LAST WEEK, WHICH HAD HER ACTING THE WAY SHE WAS AND THEN DURING OUR LAST CLASS I SAW HER BY HER LOCKER. SHE WAS JUST CRYING AND BANGING HER HANDS AGAINST THE LOCKER AND SAYING IN A SOFT VOICE WAY IS THIS HAPPENING TO ME, I HAVE NOT DONE ANYTHING WRONG I AM A GOOD DAUGHTER A GOOD PERSON WHO NEVER GETS IN TROUBLE, AND STILL ALL OF THIS HAPPENS TO ME. AND I FEEL LIKE I AM NOT WORTH ANYTHING AND AFTER WHAT MY DAD DID TO ME I CAN NOT BELIEVE I AM STILL HERE, LORD PLEASE HELP ME FIND A WAY OUT BUT NO ONE LISTENS TO ME NO ONE CARES ABOUT ME, AT THAT POINT I WALKED UP TO HER AND ASKED HER ANDREA ARE YOU OK SHE LOOKED AT ME A GAVE ME A FAKE SMILE, AND WITH TEARS IN HER EYES SHE SAID YES I AM FINE I WAS JUST REMEMBERING SOME STUFF FROM MY PAST BUT I PROMISE EVERYTHING IS OK. I DID NOT BELIEVE HER BUT ALSO, I DID NOT QUESTION HER. I FELT THAT SHE WOULD TALK WHEN SHE WAS READY, SO DID SHE EVER TALK ABOUT IT NO SHE DID NOT BUT I DID NOT WHAT TO HAVE ANY NEGATIVE THOUGHTS. WEEKS PASSED AND THE BEATINGS HAD STOPPED AND THEY HAD STOP YELLING AT HER. AND HER DAD WAS KEEPING HIS HANDS OFF HER SHE SEEMED TO STRT COMING AROUND SLOWLY, I STARTED TALKING TO HER MORE AND MORE AS FRIENDS ALWAYS AS FRIENDS NOTHING MORE, SO HER LIFE WAS GETTING BACK TOGETHER AT LESS THAT WHAT SHE THOUGHT SHE DID NOT EXPECT WHAT SHE HAD IN STORE FOR HER WHEN SHE GOT HOME AFTER SCHOOL, THAT DAY SHE SAID TO ME THANKS FOR BEING THERE FOR ME AND BEING A GOOD FRIEND AND I TOLD HER YES IT IS NOT A PROBLEM, GLAD TO BE THERE FOR YOU AS SHE WALKS AWAY AND GOES HOME THE TORTURE STARTED AGAIN HER MOM SLAPPED HER AS SOON AS SHE WALKED IN THE DOOR, AS SHE STANDS THERE CRYING HER MOM TELLS HER WHERE HAVE YOU BEEN YOUR LATE, AS SHE STANDS THERE LOOKED OVER TO THE TABLE, AND SAW HER DAD AND TWO OF HIS FRIENDS SITTING THERE WITH HIM DRINKING, AND THEY ALL LOOK AT HER UP AND DOWN, AFTERWARDS HER MOM PULLS HER HAIR AND TOLD HER GO TO YOUR ROOM AND WAIT FOR WHAT YOU HAVE COMING TO YOU, AS SHE WAS WALKING TO HER ROOM SHE WAS FULL OF TEARS AND FEAR OF WHAT WAS GOING TO HAPPEN TO HER. ANDREA WAS REMEMBERING EVERYTHING HER DAD DID TO HER IN THE PASS AS SHE GOES INTO HER ROOM, SHE OVERHEARS HER DAD FRIENDS PAYING HIM TO BE WITH HER THE FIRST MEN WALKS IN AND SAID OK YOU ARE MIND FOR AN HOUR NOW

COME HERE AND BE A GOOD GIRL, SHE SAID NO PLEASE DON'T DO THIS TO ME PLEASE I'M JUST A CHILD DON'T PLEASE STOP DON'T HURT ME THE MAN JUST LAUGH AND HAD HIS WAY WITH HER, AND THEN AFTER HE WAS DONE HE WALKED OUT AS HE WAS WALKING OUT THE NEXT MAN WALK IN AND TOLD HER OK NOW IT IS MY TURN CLEAN UP, I GOT YOU FOR AN HOUR AS SHE WAS PLEADING WITH THAT MAN NOT TO TOUCH HER, SHE LOOKED OUT HER BEDROOM DOOR AND SAW HER MOM AND DAD STANDING THERE LAUGHING AT HER. AFTER THE OTHER MAN FINISH, HE WALKED OUT SHE JUST WANTED TO DIE AS SHE WAS GETTING READY TO GO SHOWER IT HAPPENED WHAT HAPPEN MARK HER DAD WALK INTO HER ROOM NO MARK NOT HER DAD TOO. OK NOW IT IS TIME TO MAKE YOUR DADDY HAPPY HE DID WHAT HE WANTED TO DO TO HER AND AS HE DID THIS HER MOM WAS JUST LAUGHING AT HER, SHE WAS IN SO MUCH SHOCK SHE JUST STAYED SILENT NOT SAYING A WORD AS HER MOM WOULD TELL HER YOU NO GOOD NOBODY WANTS YOU, THEN AS HE LEFT HER ROOM SHE WAS IN SO MUCH PAIN SHE HAD TO GO TO THE HOSPITAL THAT NIGHT BECAUSE SHE WAS SICK AND IN LOT'S OF PAIN. AND HER PARENTS TOLD HER YOU BETTER NOT SAY NOT ONE WORD OF WHAT HAPPEN IF YOU DO, WE WILL BLAME YOUR BOYFRIEND AND HE WILL BE THE ONE GOING TO JAIL SO ANDREA LIED AT THE HOSPITAL SAYING SHE GOT RAPED BUT DID NOT KNOW WHO WERE THE BOYS THAT DID IT, SHE WAS ONLY 10 YEARS OLD WHEN ALL OF THIS WAS HAPPENING JUST A CHILD AND HAD TO DEAL WITH ALL OF THIS. NOW THERE WAS ONLY A FEW MORE WEEKS BEFORE SCHOOL WAS OVER BUT SHE DID NOT COME BACK TO SCHOOL, AT THAT POINT I NEW IT HAPPEN AGAIN BUT WHEN SHE CAME TO SCHOOL THE FOLLOWING DAY SHE SEEMED DIFFERENT SHE WAS ALWAYS HAPPY, AND I DID NOT QUESTION HER HAPPINESS AT FIRST BUT THEN I SAW HER MOOD SWING SHE WOULD BE HAPPY THEN SAD.THEN ONE DAY I WAS PASSING BY HER LOCKER AND I SAW HER SHE WAS TAKING SOME KIND OF PILLS SHE HAD GOTTEN FROM THIS PERSON IN SCHOOL, WAIT YOU TELLING ME THAT MY ANDREA IS HOOK ON DRUGS YES RANDY SHE IS ON DRUGS. AFTER ALL SHE BEEN THREW, SHE FOUND A WAY TO DEAL WITH THE LIFE THAT SHE WAS HANDED, TO HER BY HER PARENTS AND THE ABUSE CONTINUED TO HAPPEN FOR A FEW MORE YEARS, THEN FINALLY ALL THE TORTURE AND TORMENT SHE HAD EXPERIENCED FINALLY ENDED. WHEN SHE TURNED 14 YEARS OLD BUT ONE THING THAT STILL CONTINUES UP TO THIS DAY IS HER USE OF DRUGS, SHE IS STILL HOOKED ON THEM PILLS, MARK I AM SO CONFUSED OF WHAT YOU ARE SAYING WHEN I SAW HER TODAY SHE SEEMED NORMAL, SHE DID NOT SEEMED LIKE SOMEONE THAT HAS GONE THREW WHAT YOIU ARE CLAMING WHAT SHE BEEN THREW. SHE LOOKED AS IF SHE DID NOT

HAVE A CARE IN THE WORLD AS HAPPY AS ONE COULD BE, YES CAUSE EVERY MORNING SHE TAKES A PILL TO COPE WITH HER DAILY ACTIVITIES. AFTER MARK TOLD ME ALL OF THIS, I SAT ON MY BED IN TEARS NOT KNOWING WHAT I WAS GOING TO DO BUT I NEW I WAS NOT GOING TO GIVE UP ON HER, SO I WIPE MY TEARS AND FINISH GETTING READY TO GO TO ANDREA HOUSE, AS I GET TO HER HOUSE I PAUSED AND JUST LOOKED AT WHAT WAS GOING ON THE FRIENDS THAT I SAW HER WITH AT SCHOOL, WERE SITTING IN THE FRONT YARD A FEW OF THEM WERE DRINKING AND THE OTHERS WERE TAKING SOME KIND OF DRUGS. THEY LOOKED LIKE THEY WERE IN A TRANS I WALK UP TO THEM AND ASK WHERE ANDREA WAS. THEY LOOKED AT EACH OTHER AND SAID WHO ARE YOU TALKING ABOUT WHO IS THAT, WHAT DO YOU MEAN WHO IS THAT ANDREA THE GIRL THAT LIVES HERE WHERE IS SHE. AND WHO ARE YOU I AM RANDY HER BOYFRIEND, OH SO YOUR RANDY YA SHE TOLD US ABOUT YOU SHE LET'S US KNOW WHEN SHE GET'S A NEW BOYFRIEND OR GIRLFRIEND YES, SHE GOES BOTH WAYS SO TO YOUR QUESTION WHERE IS SHE, SHE IS INSIDE WITH JOSIE IT IS HER TURN THIS WEEK. BUT DON'T WORRY AFTER THE TWO OF YOU ARE TOGETHER FOR A FEW WEEKS YOU WILL GET YOUR WEEKLY TURN, WITH HER BUT HEADS UP YOU HAVE TO SUPPLY HER WITH WHAT SHE NEEDS WEEKLY OR SHE WILL STOP BEING WITH YOU AND LET YOU GO. AND WHAT DOES SHE NEED SO BADLY EVERY WEEK TELL ME DUDE YOU KNOW WHAT SHE NEEDS THESE PILLS RIGHT HERE THEY MAKE HER PAIN GO AWAY AND BRING HAPPINESS TO HER, SO HOW LONG HAS THIS BEEN GOING ON WILL IT HAS BEEN GOING ON TWO YEARS SINCE IT STARTED, BUT DON'T BE MAD AT US ALL OF THIS WAS HER IDEAL, SHE SAID I DON'T CARE ABOUT NOTHING LIFE DON'T CARE ABOUT ME SO I DON'T CARE ABOUT LIFE. IF I DIE I DIE I DON'T CARE I GIVE UP SO JUST KEEP GIVING ME THE PILLS I NEED TO BE IN MY OWN LITTLE HAPPY WORLD, AND YOU ALL CAN HAVE ME AND DO AS YOU PLEASE TO ME, AFTER PETER TOLD ME THIS I DROP TO MY KNEES AND BUSTED OUT IN TEARS, I SAT THERE ON THE GROUND FOR A BIT THEN I GOT UP AND RUSH INSIDE CALLING OUT HER NAME ANDREA MY LOVE WHERE ARE YOU I AM HERE, ANDREA ANSWER ME I HEARD CRYING IN THE ROOM NEXT TO ME I SLOWLY WALK IN AND I SAW ANDREA LAYING ON THE FLOOR, I COULD NOT BELIEVE WHAT I WAS LOOKING AT MY GIRLFRIEND ON THE FLOOR NOT RESPONDING, I ASK THE GIRL STANDING OVER HER BODY WHAT HAPPEN, WILL ANDREA SAID SHE IS TIRED OF THIS LIFE AND SHE TRY TO KILL HERSELF. BY TAKING A HAND FULL OF THESE DRUGS RIGHT HERE I AM SORRY I TRIED TO STOP HER BUT IT WAS TO LATE, I CAN NOT BELIEVE ANDREA WOULD DO SOMETHING LIKE THIS SHE WAS SO FULL OF LOVE, I GUESS ALL THE ABUSE FINALLY GOT TO HER AND IT TRIGGER A PART OF HER WHERE THERE IS NO

RETURN. I RUSHED TO HER AND DROPPED TO MY KNEES CALLING OUT TO HER ANDREA MY LOVE I AM HERE BY YOUR SIDE I PROMISE I WILL NOT LEAVE YOUR SIDE, BUT SHE COULD NOT HEAR ME SHE WAS PASSED OUT I CRIED TO HER ANDREA PLEASE DON'T DIE I LOVE YOU I STAYED BY HER SIDE TO TRY AND WAKE HER UP, I CALLED OUT TO GOD TO WAKE HER UP LORD PLEASE HELP HER AND DON'T TAKE HER FROM ME, I RUSHED AND CALLED 911 THE AMBULANCE GOT THERE WITHIN A MATTER OF MINUTES THE PARAMEDICS RUSH TO START WORKING ON HER IN THE ROOM WHERE SHE WAS IN, THEY RUSH HER TO THE HOSPITAL AS THE PARAMEDICS PUT ANDREA INTO THE AMBULANCE. I GOT IN WITH HER AND AS WE GOT TO THE HOSPITAL, THEY PLACED HER IN ONE OF THE OBSERVATION ROOMS THEY RAN ALL KINDS OF TEST ON HER AND THEN THEY PUMP HER STOMACH OUT, DURING THE OBSERVATIONS THEY NOTICE ALL THE ABUSE ON HER BODY AND HOW SHE HAS BEEN VIOLATED SO THEY CALLED THE COPS AND WITHIN AN HOUR THEY SHOWED UP. FIRST THEY QUESTIONED ME IF I KNEW WHAT HAD HAPPENDED AND I LOOKED AT THEM AND SAID NO SIR I DO NOT KNOW, STILL TRYING TO FIND OUT MYSELF SO THEY ASK ME TO STEP OUT OF THE ROOM FOR A BIT AS I WAS IN THE WAITING ROOM I SAW HER PARENTS ARRIVED, IN A RAGE DEMANDING TO TAKE HER HOME AND THAT THEY WOULD TAKE CARE OF HER, BUT THE STAFF REFUSED TO RELEASE HER SO BACK IN THE ROOM THE POLICE ASKED ANDREA VARIOUS QUESTIONS, FIRST THEY ASKED HER FOR HER NAME AND SHE SPOKE TO THEM, ASKING AM I IN TROUBLE WITH THE LAW NO ANDREA YOU ARE NOT IN TROUBLE WE ARE HERE TO HELP YOU THE DR NOTICED ALL THE ABUSED YOU HAVE BEEN IN AND WE KNOW YOU ARE SCARED TO SPEAK, BUT WE PROMISE YOU WE WILL HELP NOW WHO DID THIS TO YOU IT IS OK TELL US YOU ARE SAFE WITH US, SHE DID NOT WANT TO SAY NOTHING AS SHE STARTED TO SPEAK SHE HEARD HER PARENTS IN THE HALL SCREAMING, SO SHE CHANGE HER MIND AND DID NOT TELL THE POLICE NOTHING SO SHE LIED ABOUT WHAT HAPPENDED TO HER, AFTER A WHILE THE POLICE STOPPED QUESTIONS AND LEFT THE ROOM, SO I WENT BACK INTO THE ROOM AS LOOKED AT ANDREA I STAYED SILENT FOR A BIT THEN I ASKED HER WHAT DID YOU SAY SHE STARTED CRYING I DID NOT SAY ANYTHING, WAIT WHAT ARE YOU DOING HERE AND WHY AM I HERE WHAT HAPPEN YOU MEAN YOU DO NOT REMEMBER, WHAT YOU DID NO I DON'T TELL ME WHAT DID I DO WILL MY LOVE YOU TRYED TO KILL YOUR SELF, OH MY GOD I DO NOT REMEMBER THAT I AM GLAD THAT YOIU ARE HERE WITH ME, I THOUGHT I LOST YOU I AM GLAD THAT YOU DID NOT LEAVE ME, I LOVE YOU RANDY I LOVE YOU TOO. LOOKED ANDREA I KNOW WHAT HAPPEN TO YOU IN THE PASS MARK TOLD ME EVERYTHING WHAT YOUR PARENTS DID TO YOU, AS I SAID THIS HER PARENTS WALK IN ACTING AS IF

THEY CARED AND THEY TOLD ME YOU CAN GO NOW WE ARE HERE, NO HE IS NOT GOING NO WHERE HE WAS THERE FOR ME HE SAVED MY LIFE HE IS NOT LEAVING IF ANYONE IS LEAVING IT IS THE BOTH OF YALL, RANDY IT IS YOUR FAULT SHE IS LIKE THIS WHAT DO YOU MEAN IT IS MY FAULT, I HELPED TO SAVE HER LIFE WHERE WERE YOU WHEN SHE NEEDED A PARENT TO LOOK OVER HER, DON'T YOU QUESTION US WE DO NOT HAVE TO ANSWERE TO YOU ANDREA SPOKE IT IS NOT HIS FAULT HE SAVED MY LIFE, AND THEY LOOKED AT ME AND SAID YES EXACTLY IT'S HIS FAULT YOU ARE STILL ALIVE, HE RUINED EVERYTHING SO I LEFT BUT DID NOT GIVE UP ON HER I'M ALWAYS BY HER SIDE NEVER STOP CARING FOR HER. THE FOLLOWING DAY ANDREA WAS RELEASED FROM THE HOSPITAL I WENT TO GO SEE HER AND HOW SHE WAS DOING, AS ANDREA CAME OUT OF HER HOUSE IN TEARS I ASKED HER WHATS WRONG TELL ME, WILL MY PARENTS ARE SENDING ME TO GO STAY WITH MY AUNT WHICH I HAD NEVER MET, NEVER KNEW SHE EXISTED AND I WAS IN SHOCK AS SHE WAS TELLING ME THIS, ANDERA I WILL NEVER SEE YOU AGAIN RANDY YOU WILL SEE ME AGAIN, I PROMISE YOU I WILL NEVER LEAVE YOU WE WILL BE TOGETHER FOREVER. I WILL JUST BE GONE FOR A WHILE, BUT THE CRAZY THING ABOUT THIS MY PARENTS SAID DO NOT BELIEVE WHAT GRANDMA TELL'S ME THAT SHE LIKES TO LIE ALOT SO WHEN IT COMES TO US IT WILL BE NOTHING BUT LIES, BUT FOR SOME STRANGE REASON I BELIEVE THAT WHAT GRANDMA WILL TELL ME, WILL BE THE WHOLE TRUTH ABOUT MY PARENTS SO I TOLD HER WOW THAT IS CRAZY, SO WHEN ARE YOU LEAVING TO YOUR AUNT;S HOUSE I WILL BE GOING THIS WEEKEND THEY ARE GOING TO DRIVE ME TO MY GRANDMA'S HOUSE. YOU KNOW RANDY I NEVER THOUGHT I WOULD FINALLY MAKE IT OUT OF THIS HOUSE BUT I PRAYED AND PRAYED, AND HOPE THAT GOD WOULD ANSWER MY PRAYERS AND TAKE ME OUT OF THIS HOUSE. AND MY PRAYERS WERE ANSWER. RANDY I GOT TO TELL YOU SOMETHING WHAT IS IT ANDREA, DO YOU KNOW I HAD SO MANY THOUGHTS OF GOING TO MY PARENTS ROOM AT NIGHT AND ENDING THEIR LIVES BUT I NEVER DID CAUSE I WANT THEM TO PAY THE RIGHT WAY I WANT THERE SUFFERING TO LAST A LONG TIME, LIKE THEY MADE ME SUFFER FOR SO MANY YEARS BUT I THANK GOD FOR EVERYTHING HE HAS DONE FOR ME AND I KNOW IT IS BEACUSE OF HIS GRACE THAT I MADE IT OUT ALIVE. AND FROM THIS DAY FORWARD EVRYTHING IS GOING TO BE OK , THERE IS NOTHING THAT COULD MAKE ME SAD OR FEEL PAIN NO MORE I AM FINALLY SET FREE.

CHAPTER 3   DEEP SECRETS

IT IS GOING TO BE A RELIFE TO GET AWAY FROM THIS AS SHE TURNS TO GO BACK INTO HER HOUSE, SHE STOPS ON THE WAY IN AS SHE STANDS ON THE PORCH WITH TEARS IN HER EYES NOT SAYING A WORD, JUST LOOKING DOWN THEN SHE SAY'S RANDY DO YOU KNOW HOW IT FEELS TO GET ABUSED EVERY DAY OF YOUR LIFE. FOR NO REASON BEATINGS IN THE MORNING, AND THEN AT NIGHT HAVING YOUR DAD AND HIS FRIENDS ALL OVER YOU, MY DAD TOOK MY INNOCENCE AWAY FROM ME THAT IS SOMETHING I CAN NEVER GET BACK, ANDREA WAS IN SO MANY TEARS AND SAID I WAS ONLY A LITTLE GIRL HOW CAN THE PARENTS OF A LITLE GIRL BRING SO MUCH PAIN AND SUFFERING TO THEIR CHILD. I THOUGHT PARENTS ARE SUPPOSED TO BE LOVING AND CARING BRINGING HAPPINESS TO THEIR CHILDREN, NOT PAIN AND SUFFERING I DO NOT UNDERSTAND THIS, DID I DO SOMETHING WRONG WAS I NOT SUPPOSED TO HAVE BEEN BORN, I LOOK AROUND ME EVERYDAY AND SEE ALL THE OTHER KIDS MY AGE, THEY ARE HAPPY WITH THEIR PARENTS AT THE MALL AND AT THE PARK. THEIR PARENTS BUYING THEM GIFTS JUST HAPPY FAMILIES BUT MY PARENTS ALL THEY DID WAS BUY DRUGS AND ALCOHOL, AND IF THEY RAN OUT OF MONEY THEN MY DAD WOULD COME INTO MY ROOM AND HIT ME THEN HE WOULD CALL HIS FRIENDS TO COME OVER AND WOULD GIVE HIM MONEY, THEN THEY WOULD ALL JUST SIT THERE AND USE ME AND ABUSE ME AND LAUGH. RANDY ONE DAY I WILL GET MY REDEMPTION ON THEM LOOK I AM SORRY I HAVE TO GO I WILL TALK TO YOU LATER I LOVE YOU, AS SHE WALKED INSIDE ALL I COULD DO WAS STAND THERE SPEECHLESS WITH TEARS IN MY EYES WITHOUT A WORD TO SAY AND LOT'S OF PAIN IN MY HEART FOR HER ALL I COULD DO WAS JUST THINK ABOUT ALL SHE HAD BEEN THROUGH, THERE HAS TO BE MORE THAN WHAT IS GOING ON HOW COULD SOME ONE TREAT THEIR CHILD LIKE THAT FOR NO REASON. I WILL DO WHATEVER I CAN AND DO MY MY BEST TO FIND A WAY OUT FOR ANDREA AND I WILL NOT REST UNTIL SHE GETS HER PAY BACK FOR WHAT THEY DID TO HER, WILL TOMORROW IS SATURDAY AND ANDERA WILL BE LEAVING ME TO GO TO HER AUNT'S HOUSE WHICH SHE HAD NEVER SEEN BEFORE OR NEW ABOUT, WE WILL SEE HOW THAT GOES I WILL PRAY FOR HER AS I GET HOME I AM JUST THINKING ABOUT EVERYTHING. THAT WAS REVIEW TO ME AND ALL THAT HAPPENED TO ANDREA SO TONIGHT I

WILL JUST WAIT AND HOPE FOR A SOLUTION, FOR HER SHE DOES NOT DESERVES THIS I WILL GO SEE HER EARLY IN THE MORNING BEFORE SHE LEAVES, I WILL GO TO SLEEP NOW AND WAKE UP EARLY IN THE MORNING AND GO SEE ANDREA FOR THELAST TIE. UNTIL I DO NOT KNOW WHEN AS I SLEEP, I FOUND MYSELF IN A DREAM ABOUT HER IN MY DREAMS WE WERE AS HAPPY AS WE COLD BE, NOT A WORRY IN THE WORLD EVERYTHING WAS GREAT, AS RANDY LAY IN HIS BED TO SLEEP ALL HE COULD THINK AND DREAM ABOUT WAS HIS TRUE LOVE ANDREA. HE COULD SEE THE PAIN THAT SHE HAS BEEN GOING THREW ALL THESE YEARS AT THAT POINT RANDY DID NOT UNDERSTAND EVERYTHING, THAT WAS GOING ON BUT HE NEW THAT SOMETHING GOOD WILL COME OUT OF ALL OF THIS, MORNING IS NEAR LET'S SEE HOW RANDY WILL RESPOND AS HE WAKS UP TO GO TO ANDREA HOUSE FOR THE LAST TIME. HE IS SO SAD FROM KNOWING HE WILL NOT SEE HIS GIRLFRIEND AGAIN FOR NOT KNOWING HOW LONG, AFTER TODAY EVERYTHING GREAT WILL BE MISSING FROM RANDY'S LIFE AS RANDY WOKE UP, HE WAS BROUGHT BACK INTO REALITY THAT IS HAPPENING AT THIS PRESENT MOMENT. WILL IM READY BUT NOT READY TO GO TO ANDREA HOUSE KNOWING THIS WILL BE THE LAST TIME THAT I SEE HER, BRINGS A DEEP EMPTYNESS TO MY HEART WHICH I CAN NOT STAND I DO NOT KNOW HOW I WILL RESPOND WHEN ANDREA GIVES ME THE LAST GOODBYE KISS AND HUG I KNOW THIS WILL BE THE LAST TIME I SEE HER UNTIL SHE RETURNS BACK TO ME, I KNOW I AM GOING TO MISS HER SO MUCH AS I AM WALKING TO HER HOUSE EVERY STEP I TAKE REMINDS ME OF HOW WE USED TO WALK DOWN THOSES STREETS. AND NOW FROM THIS DAY FORWARD WHEN I WALK DOWN THESE STREETS, I WILL BE WALKING THEM ALONE WITHOUT MY PARTNER BY MY SIDE WILL I MADE IT TO ANDERA HOUSE AS I TAKE A DEEP BREATH, I SEE HER WALK OUT THE DOOR AS SOON AS I SEE HER TEARS START FALLING FROM MY EYES, SHE STANDS THERE FOR A MOMENT AND I SEE THE PAIN IN HER EYES AS TEARS FALL TO THE FLOOR, AS SHE SLOWLY WALKS DOWN THOSES STEPS SHE STOPS ON THE LAST STEP, AND I GO UP TO HER AND HOLD HER TIGHT IN MY ARMS KNOWING THIS WILL BE THE LAST TIME I HOLD HER I DID NOT WANT TO LET GO. I WAS JUST CRYING LIKE A BABY KNOWING SHE WOULD NOT BE AROUND NO MORE, AS I LOOK INTO HER EYES, I FINALLY SPEAK BABY I LOVE YOU AND I WILL ALWAYS BE HERE WAITING FOR YOU I LOVE YOU RANDY I DON'T WANT TO LEAVE YOU BUT PLEASE UNDERSTAND I HAVE TO GO FOR A WHILE I HAVE TO FIND WHO I AM, WHAT YOU MEAN WHO YOU ARE YOU ARE MY TRUE LOVE ANDREA, RANDY YOU KNOW WHAT I MEAN YES I KNOW I AM JUST SO LOST KNOWING I WILL BE HERE WITHOUT YOU RANDY I HAVE BEEN LOST ALL OF THESE YEARS, I NEED A NEW START BUT I PROMISE YOU THAT WE

WILL ONLY BE SEPARATED A FEW MONTHS, I HAVE TO GO NOW BUT I WILL ALWAYS HAVE YOU IN MY HEART AND I WILL ALWAYS LOVE YOU, AND KEEP YOU IN MY PRAYERS I LOVE YOU ANDREA I LOVE YOU PLEASE HURRY AND COME BACK TO ME I WILL BE BACK WHEN THE TIME IS RIGHT, AS I TOLD ANDREA MY LAST GOOD BYES I LEFT HER HOUSE WITH MY HEAD LOOKING DOWN JUST AS SAD AS I COULD BE, I HATED TO LEAVE RANDY LIKE THIS. IT BROKE MY HEART TO SEE HIM SO SAD THE SAD LOOK ON HIS FACE WILL ALWAYS BE IN MY THOUGHTS; I KNOW HE WAS SO HURT AND HIS HEART WAS TORNED INTO LITTLE PIECES I FEEL THE SAME PAIN AS HE DOES, I PROMISE WE WILL BE BACK TOGETHER REAL SOON AS I WILL BE AT MY AUNT' HOUSE IN A FEW HOURS, AND HOPEFULLY SHE WILL TELL ME THE TRUTH ABOUT WHAT REALLY IS GOING ON IN MY FAMILY WHY MY PARENTS TREATED ME THE WAY THEY DID. PUTTING ME THREW ALL THAT PAIN AND SUFFERING FOR NO REASON, IT'S GOING TO BE ALONG RIDE TO MY AUNT'S HOUSE AS WE ARE ON THIS LONELY ROAD I LOOK OUT THE WINDOW. AS I SEE ALL THE MOUNTAINS AND RIVERS AROUND, I CLOSED MY EYE'S FOR A MOMENT AND STARTED THINKING I WISH I COULD JUST DISAPPEAR INTO THOSES MOUNTAINS BUT OVERALL IT WAS A VERY BEAUTIFUL SIGHT. FOR THAT MOMENT I WISH I COULD HAVE BEEN AS FREE AS THOSES TREES AND MY LIFE AS CALM AS THE RIVER BUT THAT WAS NOT MY LIFE FOR THE MOMENT, THREW THE WHOLE TRIP I WAS TRYING TO FIND MY INNER PEACE BUT IT IS HARD WHEN I HAVE MORE TRAUMA THAN PEACE, I HAVE COME TO REALIZE THAT I NEED A NEW START IN M LIFE I MUST START THE RECOVERY PHASE, A FEW MORE HOURS AND WE WILL ARRIVE AT MY AUNT'S HOUSE. I AM GLAD I AM FINALLY GOING TO GET TO KNOW ALL OF MY FAMILY, BUT UNFORTUNATELY ALL I KNEW IN MY LIFE WAS TORTURE AND THAT PART OF MY LIFE WHICH WAS FULL OF PAIN, AND SUFFERING WHICH WAS HANDED TO ME BY MY PARENTS. BUT THOSE DAYS ARE OVER WITH, NOW THE SCARES WILL ALWAYS BE ON MY BODY AND IN MY HEART AND I WILL USE THEM AS A REMINDER OF HOW LIFE REALLY IS, I WILL MAKE IT MY LIFE JOURNEY THAT ANOTHER CHILD NEVER GOES THREW WHAT I WENT THREW, WITH TIME THE INNER PART OF ME WILL REGROW TO BE A STRONGER AND BETTER PERSON FULL OF LOVE AND HAPPINESS, AS WE MY AUNT'S HOUSE I CLOSED MY EYES FOR A BIT AND PRAY THAT SHE WOULD BE THE SWEETEST PERSON IN THE WORLD AND TREAT ME RIGHT, I SAW MY WHOLE LIFE FLASH IN FRONT OF ME AS IF I WAS WATCHING A HORROR MOVIE. I THANK GOD FOR TAKING ME OUT OF SITUATION I WAS IN I LOOK OUT THE WINDOW, AND SAW MY AUNT STANDING ON THE PORCH AS I WAS LOOKING AT HER WAS LIKE LOOKING AT MY MOM, I WAS STARTING TO GET SCARED BUT THEN I REALIZE I WOULD BE OK WITH HER, THERE WAS ANOTHER OLDER LADY STANDING NEXT

TO HER I ASK MY SO CALLED PARENTS WHO WAS THAT LADY, THEY STAYED SILENT FOR A MOMENT THEN THEY SAID SHE IS YOUR GRANDMA, MY GRANDMA WOW SHE IS VERY BEAUTIFUL I GOT OUT OF THE CAR AND STOOD THERE FOR A MOMENT AS I COULD NOT WALK, THEN I SLOWLY STARTED WALKING TOWARDS THEM NOT KNOWING WHAT TO EXPECT. AS I STOOD THERE IN FRONT OF THEM MY AUNT LOOKED AT ME AND WITH A BIG SMILE ON HER FACE, SHE SAID YOUR JUST A BABY AS SHE SAID THIS, SHE WALK OFF THE PORCH AND GAVE ME THE BIGGEST HUG FULL OF LOVE AT THAT POINT I NEW I WAS FINALLLY HOME THEN SHE TOLD ME I BEEN WAITING MANY YEARS TO SEE YOU AS SHE SAID THIS TEARS ROLL FROM MY EYES, SHE ASKED WHY ARE YOU CRYING IT IS JUST THAT I BEEN WANTING TO KNOW MY FAMILY BUT MY PARENTS WOULD NOT LET ME MEET NO ONE. SO YOU DON'T KNOW YOUR FAMILY NO I DON'T AS I SAID THIS, I TURN TO THE OTHER LADY ARE YOU MY GRANDMA, YES MIJA I AM YOUR GRANDMA SHE CAME UP TO ME AND GAVE ME A BIG HUG. AS I WAS STANDING THERE IN TEARS IN FRONT OF THEM, I TURN BACK AND SAW MY SO-CALLED PARENTS DRIVE OFF AS THEY DID, I TOOK A DEEP BREATH OF RELIFE FINALLY THEY ARE GONE OUT OF MY LIFE I PRAY I NEVER SEE THEM AGAIN, NOW I SHALL REST THEN FIND OUT THE TRUTH ABOUT EVERYTHING, WHICH WILL HAPEN AT THE RIGHT TIME, AS MY AUNT ASKED ME IF I WAS HUNGRY I SMILED AND LOOK AT HER YES TIA I AM SO HUNGRY RIGHT NOW, OK DINNER WILL BE READY SOON AND IF YOU NEED ANYTHNG LET US KNOW WE LOVE YOU AND WE ARE HERE FOR YOU TO MAKE YOU HAPPY, AS MY AUNT TOLD ME THIS I STARTED CRYING BUT HAPPY TEARS. AS MY AUNT SAW ME CRYING, SHE CAME UP TO ME AND ASK WHATS WRONG NO NOTHING IS WRONG THEN WHAT IS IT, TIA THIS IS THE FIRST TIME IN MY LIFE THAT SOMEONE BESIDES MY BOYFRIEND TOLD ME THEY LOVE ME AND CARE ABOUT MY HAPPINESS, WILL AS I SAID WE ARE HERE FOR YOU LOOK ANDREA THERE IS MUCH I HAVE TO TELL YOU ABOUT YOUR MOM AND DAD, BUT I WILL SAVE THAT CONVERSATION FOR ANOTHER DAY, RIGHT NOW I WANT YOU TO GO TO YOUR ROOM AND SEE WHAT WE GOY YOU, WAIT YOU GOT ME A GIFT? YES, JUST GO AND SEE WHAT WE GOT YOU HOPE YOU LIKE IT AS I WALK AWAY, I COULD NOT HELP IT TEARS JUST KEPT FALLING FROM MY EYES I WAS SO CONFUSED AT THE SAME TIME. SO, I STOP AND TURN AROUND TIA WHY AER YOU BING SO NICE TO ME NOT EVEN KNOWING ME AND SHE SMILED, AND SAID YOU ARE FAMILY ADN YOU ALWAYS TREAT FAMILY RIGHT AND SHOW THEM LOVE AND HAPPINESS. WHEN I HEARD THOSE WORDS, I WAS SO LOST FOR WORDS I DID NOT KNOW WHAT TO SAY I JUST WENT UP TO HER AND GAVE HER A BIG HUG. OK NOW GO SEE WHAT WE GOT YOU AS I OPEN THE DOOR TO MY NEW ROOM, I SAW ON MY BED A BIG BEAR FLOWERS AND A BIG BOX OF CHOCOLATE

CANDY ALONG WITH CLOTHES AND PERFUME. WHEN I SAW THIS, I FAIL TO MY KNEES AND RAISE MY HANDS TO GOD WITH A BIG THANKFUL HEART AND TEARS I PRAY THANK YOU JESUS CHRIST FOR BRINGING ME TO A HOUSE FULL OF LOVE AND HAPPINESS, I ALWAYS NEW IN MY HEART YOU WOULD TAKE CARE OF YOUR CHILDREN I LOVE YOU JESUS CHRIST AMEN, AS I GO BACK INTO THE KITCHEN I LOOK AT MY AUNT AND GRANDMA THEY WERE BOTH STANDING THERE WITH A BIG SMILE ON THERE FACE. SO DID YOU LIKE THE GIFTS YES, I LOVE ALL THE GIFTS THANK YOU BOTH SO MUCH, AS I SAT AT THE TABLE I LOOKED DOWN AND I TOLD THEM YOU KNOW AT MY PARENTS HOUSE THEY WERE NOT EXACTLY GOOD PARENTS THEY WERE EVIL. THEY NEVER SHOWED ME LOVE ALL THEY SHOWED ME WAS PAIN AND SUFFERING, THEY NEVER TOLD ME THEY LOVED ME THEY NEVER DID ANYTHING NICE FOR ME. ALL THEY DID WAS USE ME AND ABUSE ME AND LAUGHAT ALL MY SUFFERING. I CRYED SO MANY NIGHTS IN MY ROOM ASKING GOD TO TAKE ME AWAY FROM THAT EVIL HOUSE AND HE ANSWER MY PRAYERS, MY POOR CHILD I KNEW SOMETHING WAS NOT RIGHT WITH THEM, ONCE YOU ARE SETTLED IN GOOD THEN WE ARE GOING THEN WE ARE GOING TO HAVE A LONG TALK WITH YOU ABOUT YOUR PARENTS, AS I LOOKED AT HER I TOLD HER YES, I HAVE LOT'S OF QUESTIONS I AM NOT READY FOR THIS RIGHT NOW I WILL LET YOUKNOW WHEN I AM READY TO TALK ABOUT MR. AND MRS. GARCIA. I DO NOT CONSIDER THEM MY PARENTS TO ME THEY ARE MONSTERS THEN MY GRANDMA SAID OK MIJA WHEN YOU ARE READY, WE WILL ALSO BE READY THANKS GRANDMA THE ONLY CONCERN THAT IS DEEP IN MY HEART I STILL HAVE NOT SPOKEN TO RANDY, I PROMISE HIM I WOULD CALL HIM AND I STILL HAVE NOT YET I HOPE HE IS OK I KNOW HE MISSES ME AS MUCH AS I MISS HIM, I HOPE I CAN GO BACK TO HIM SOON AS I WALK INTO THE KITCHEN I SEE MY AUNT JOSIE AND MY GRANDMA SITTING AT THE TABLE RINKING A CUP OF COFFEE, AS THEY SEE I WALKED INTHEY PAUSED AND ASKED ME IF EVERYTHING WAS OK, YES EVERYTHING IS GREAT I JUST WANT TO LET YOU KNOW THAT I AM READY TO TALK ABOUT THOSES PEOPLE, AS I SAID THIS THEY LOOKED AT EACH OTHER AND LOOK UP AT ME AND SAID OK MIJA LET ME MAKE YOU SOMETHING TO EAT, THEN WE WILL TALK I TOOK A DEEP BREATH OK TIA SOUNDS GOOD AS I SAT DOWN AT THE TABLE THEY STARTED TELLING ME EVERYTHING, OK ANDREA I REMEMBER WHEN YOUR DAD FIRST CAME TO OUR HOUSE, HE WAS DATING MY DAUGHTER SANDRA THEN I SAID WAIT THAT IS NOT MY MOM NAME. HER NAME IS YVETTE I KNOW BUT HOLD ON THERE IS ALOT MORE TO THIS STORY SEE YOUR DAD AND MY DAUGHTER HAD JUST GOTTEN TOGETHER, AND THEY TRYED SO MANY TIMES TO HAVE KIDS MY DAUGHTER COULD NOT HAVE KIDS SO HE LEFT HER, AND GOT TOGETHER WITH ANOTHER

WOMAN SHE GAVE BIRTH TO A GIRL SO I ASKED HER IF IT WAS ME NO THT WAS YOUR OLDER SISTER, SO SHE STAYED WITH YOUR DAD UNTIL YOUR SISTER TURNED 15 YEARS OLD. THEN HE LEFT HER, AS GRANDMA SAID THIS, SHE LOOK AT ME WITH THE SADDEST EYES GRANDMA WHAT IS IT TELL ME SHE LOOKED AT ME THEN LOOKED DOWN AND SAID YOUR OLDER SISTER IS YOUR MOM. WHEN SHE TOLD ME THIS, I WAS IN SHOCK WAIT HOW CAN THIS BE THEY NEVER TOLD ME ANYTHING. SO, WHAT ABOUT MY BROTHER ALEX ARE THEY HIS PARENTS YES, HE IS THEIR SON, ANDREA YOUR DAD IS AN EVIL PERSON AND HE TURNED YOUR SISTER INTO AN EVIL PERSON TOO SHE IS FULL OF HATE AND LOVES TO SEE PEOPLE GET HURT, THAT IS WHY THEY TREATED YOU THE WAY THEY DID AS SHE FINISH SPEAKING I LOOKED AT HER AS I SAID I DON'T WANT TO HEAR NO MORE I GOT UP FROM THE TABLE AND RAN TO MY ROOM IN TEARS, I CLOSED MY EYES AND LOOK FOR RANDY IN MY THOUGHTS FOR HE IS THE ONLY ONE THAT CAN MAKE ME FEEL BETTER, I CRYED MY HEART OUT ALL NIGHT THIS TORE ME UP, I AM READY TO GO BACK HOME I NEED TO LEAVE I WILL REST TONIGHT AND GO EARLY IN THE MORNING. I MISS MY FRIENDS AND RANDY SO MUCH I NEED TO GO TO MY HOMETOWN, I MUST TALK TO RANDY AND LET HIM KNOW ABOUT ALL THAT I LEARNED AS I WAS HERE AS I WALK INTO THE KITCHEN TO TELL MY TIA AND GRANDMA THAT I MUST LEAVE FOR A WHILE AND GO BACK HOME TO FAIL CHARGES ON MY MOM AND DAD FOR EVERYTHING THEY DID TO ME. MY MOM FOR LETTING HIM DO THESE THINGS TO ME, AS I TOLD MY AUNT AND GRANDMA WHAT I WAS INTENDING ON DOING I SAW TEARS COMING OUT OF MY AUNTS EYES, TIA DON'T CRY I WILL BE BACK I PROMISE REMEMBER WE ARE FAMILY AND FAMILY ALWAYS MAKE SURE WE ARE HAPPY, AFTER I TOLD MY AUNT THIS SHE JUST SMILED I REALLY ENJOY EVERY SECOND I WAS HERE, THE DAY'S I HAVE BEEN HERE YOU BOTH SHOWED ME MORE LOAVE AND HAPPINESS THEN THEY SHOW ME ALL MY LIFE, WHEN I GET EVERYTHING SETTLE I WILL COME BACK I PROMISE. NOW TOMORROW I WILL BE LEAVING AS I WALKED OUT OF THE ROOM, I STOP AT THE DOOR YOU KNOW WHAT TIA? WHAT IS IT MIJA FOR YEARS I WOULD ASK MYSELF WHY I GOT TREATED THE WAY I DID, WHY DON'T THEY LOVE ME THEY LOOK AT ME WITH ALOT OF HATE, AS IF I DID SOMETHING WRONG, I ALWAYS THOUGHT IT WAS MY FAULT FOR THE WAY, THEY WOULD TREATED ME. NOW I COME TO REALIZE THAT THE WHOLE TIME IT WAS THEM THAT DID WRONG, I KNOW IT IS WRONG TO SAY BUT I HATE THEM I HOPE I NEVER SEE THEM AGAIN. THEY WERE BOTH LOST FOR WORDS SO THEY JUST STAYED THERE SILENT AS THEY LOOKED INTO MY EYES AND SAW ALL I BEEN GOING THREW, I COULD NOT SPEAK NO MORE I JUST TURNED PUT MY HEAD DOWN AND WALKED TOWARDS MY ROOM, I WILL LAY AND REST FOR I MUST

PREPARED FOR TOMORROW I KNOW RANDY WILL BE SURPRISED WHEN I SEE HIM, I MUST TELL HIM EVERYTHING THAT IS GOING ON AS I WAS FALLING ASLEEP I HEARD MY AUNT AND GRANDMA TALKING IN THE KITCHEN, AS THEY WERE TALKING I HEARD FOOTSTEPS IN THE HALL COMING TOWARDS MY ROOM. THE DOOR OPENED SLOWLY AS I SAW MY DOOR OPEING I GOT SCARED AND STARTED SCREAMING, ANDREA IT IS ME I AM SORRY WHEN THE DOOR SLOWLY OPEN IT BROUGHT BACK MEMORIES OF HOW MY PARENTS WOULD COME INTO MY ROOM, AT NIGHT AND DESTROYED MY LIFE AS I WAS SPEAKING MY GRANDMA WAS JUST STANDING THERE SAYING SHE IS SO BEAUTIFUL JUST A BABY. MY HEART GOES OUT TO HER SHE DOES NOT DESERVE THIS TREATMENT; I LOVE HER AS MY OWN DAUGHTER I PRAY SHE DOES COME BACK AS SHE PROMISE SHE WOULD THEN THEY LEFT MY ROOM I FELT SO BLESSED THERE AT THERE HOUSE, I LISTEN IN AS MY GRANDMA TOLD MY AUNT I AM GOING TO MISS HER SO MUCH I ALWAYS WANTED A DAUGHTER AS PRECIOUS AS SHE IS, SHE IS SUCH A PRECIOUS PERSON FOR HER TO SUFFER AS SHE DID THAT IS NOT RIGHT, I PRAY WHEN SHE GET'S BACK SHE MAKES THEM PAY FOR ALL THE PAIN THEY HAD CAUSED HER. AND I AM GOING TO SEE TO IT MYSELF THAT JUSTICE IS BROUGHT FOR ANDREA SHE CAME TO US AS A GIFT FROM GOD TO HELP AND PROTECT AND THAT IS WHAT WE WILL DO IS HELP HER AND PROTECT HER, GOOD MORNING ANDREA HOW DID YOU SLEEP I SLEPT WILL GRANDMA. HOW ABOUT YOU HOW DID YOU SLEEP NOT SO WILL MIJA ALL I COULD DO WAS THINK ABOUT YOU LEAVING US TODAY, OH GRANDMA DON'T WORRY I WILL BE BACK SONNER THAN YOU THINK I JUST HAVE TO GO BACK AND TAKE CARE OF WHAT NEEDS TOBE TAKEN CARE OF, AND WHEN I COME BACK IS IT OK IF I BRING RANDY BACK WITH ME. YES MIJA I WOULD LOVE TO MEET HIM DO YALL PLAN ON GETTING MARRIED? GRANDMA I DON'T WE HAVE NOT TALK ABOUT THAT EVERYTHING THAT BEEN GOING ON BUT I AM SURE WE WILL GET MARRIED ONE DAY, IS YOUR PARENTS GOING TO COME BACK AND PICK YOU UP? OH NO IT IS A SURPRISE VISIT THEY NOT EXPECTING ME BACK, NEXT TIME THEY SEE ME I WILL HAVE THE COPS WITH ME THEN AS THE COPS TAKE THEM TO JAIL, I WILL BE THE ONE LAUGHING AT THEM. SO HOW ARE YOU GOING HOME I AM GOING TO TAKE THE BUS I SHOULD BE BACK IN ROSENBERG IN LIKE 4 HOURS, MY BUS WILL BE LEAVING IN 2 HOURS SO I NEED TO HURRY AND PACK SO I CAN BE ON TIME AT THE BUS STATION, AS I WALKED AWAY TO GO GRAB MY BAGS I TRUNED AND LOOKED AT MY GRANDMA AND TIA SARA, THEY WERE BOTH STNDING THERE WITH TEARS OF IN THERE EYES THEY HAD THE SADDEST LOOK ON THERE FACE. I WENT UP TO THE BOTH OF THEM AS I HUG THEM I WHISPER IN THERE EARS I LOVE YOU BOTH VERY MUCH PLEASE DON'T CRY I WILL BE BACK SOON, AS I

GRAB MY STUFF I WALK TO THE FRONT DOOR I STAND BY THE DOOR TURNED AND TOLD THEM BOTH I LOVE YOU BOTH VERY MUCH BYE, AS I WALKED TO THE BUS STATION WHICH WAS A FEW BLOCKS AWAY ALL I COULD DO WAS THINK ABOUT MY BOYFRIEND RANDY AND HOW MUCH I MISSED HIM AND LOVE HIM AS I GET TO THE BUS STATION I STOP AT THE ENTRANCE TO THE BUS STATION WITH MY HAND ON THE DOOR, I STAND THERE FOR A BIT AND STARTED THINKING WHAT IF RANDY LEFT ME FOR NOT CALLING HIM FOR 6 MONTHS, AND FOUND ANOTHER GIRLFRIEND OR WHEN I GET BACK HE TELLS ME HE DOSE NOT WANT ME NO MORE, THAT I HAVE BEEN GONE SO LONG THAT HE LOST HIS LOVE FOR ME. NO I CAN NOT LOOSE HIM I NEED TO HURRY AND GET BACK HOME, AND LEET HIM KNOW HOW MUCH I LOVE HIM AND MISS HIM, BUT I KNOW EVERYTHNKG WILL BE OK I AM JUST OVER THNKING EVERYTHNG, NOW I MUST GO GET MY TICKET AS I GET TO THE COUNTER THE MAN ASK SO WHERE ARE YOU GOING TO? I SMILED ONE WAY TO ROSENBERG TEXAS PLEASE, OK HERE IS YOUR TICKET THE BUS WILL ARRIVE SHORTLY THANK YOU, I LOOKED AT THE CLOCK AS I GOT MY BAGS I WAITED FOR THE BUS TO GET THERE, WHICH WAS THE LONGEST WAIT EVER I WAS JUST SO EXCITED TO GO BACK TO ROSENBERG THAT EVERY SECOND FELT LIKE AN HOUR. AS I STOOD THERE FOR A BIT JUST LOOKING INTO MY PAST AND ALL I COULD DO WAS CRY, FOR THE PAIN I HAD INSIDE OF ME WAS BREAKING MY HEART AND MY LIFE IS FULL OF ALOT OF BROKEN DREAMS I DID NOT KNOW WHAT MY LIFE WAS GOING TO BE FROM THAT DAY FORWARD. ALL I NEW AS LONG AS I HAD RANDY IN MY LIFE I WOULD BE OK I JUST PRAY THAT WHEN I GET BACK HE WILL BE THERE WAITING FOR ME, WE PROMISE EACH OTHER THAT WE WOULD BE TOGETHER UNTIL IT IS TIME TO REST AS I STOOD THERE I LOOKED ALL AROUND ME ALL I SAW WAS HAPPY FAMILIES, JUST SMILING AND HUGGING EACH OTHER SAYING I LOVE YOU, WHY CAN'T I GET THAT KIND OF RESPONSE. WHY DO PEOPLE HATE ME I ALWAYS GET THE WORST OUR OF EVERYONE, THAT IS WHY I CAN NOT LOOSE RANDY HE IS THE ONLY ONE BESIDE MY AUNT AND GRANDMA THAT SHOWED ME TRUE LOVE, I KNOW WHEN I GET BACK I HAVE ALOT OF EXPLAINING TO DO I JUST HOPE RANDY BELIEVES ME WHEN I TELL HIM WHAT I NEED TO TELL HIM, ALL OF THIS HAPPENED TO ME AND IT IS HARD FOR ME TO BELIEVE IT SO HOW CAN I EXPECT RANDY TO BELIEVE ME, I HOPE IT ALL GOES WILL I KNOW THAT WHATEVER HAPPENS I WILL ALWAYS LOVE HIM AND SHOW HIM LOVE, AS THESE PERPLE SHOWED LOVE TO EACH OTHER WILL IT IS TIME TO GO I SEE MY BUS PULLING UP, ANDREA WAS GETTING READY TO BOARD THE BUS TO GO BACK TO HER HOMETOWN TO FACE THE PEOPLE THAT DESTROYED HER LIFE IN THAT VIOLENT HOME, SHE KNOW WHEN SHE GOT AS ANDREA LOOKS LOST SHE IS SCARED TO

MEET UP WITH HER PARENTS AGAIN. ANDREA WILL BE HOME SOON AND SHE STILL DOES NOT KNOW THAT RANDY IS IN THE HOSPITAL IN A COMA WHAT WILL HER REACTION BE WHEN SHE GETS HOME AND FINDS RANDY IS IN THE HOSPITAL, ANDREA HEARS HER NAME CALLED ON THE LOUD SPEAKER TO GO TO THE SERVICE DESK SHE HAS A PHONE CALL HELLO I AM ANDREA I HAVE A CALL YES, HELLO IM ANDREA WHO SPEAKING HELLO ANDREA IT IS ME JUDY HEY JUDY HOW DID YOU KNOW I WOULD BE HERE, I HEARD YOU WERE COMING BACK TODAY I WAS SHOCKED THAT SHE NEW I WAS RETURNING TODAY SO WHO TOLD YOU I HAVE MY WAYS OF FINDING OUT. BUT LOOKED WE NEED TO HAVE A SERIOUS TALK I WILL BE AT THE BUS STATION WAITING FOR YOU I WILL PICK YOU UP, AS ANDREA HUNG UP THE PHONE SHE STAYED THERE FOR A MOMENT WITH HER HAND ON THE PHONE WONDERING WHAT WAS SO IMPORANT THAT SHE HAS TO PICK ME UP, AS ANDREA WENT BACK TO HER SEAT SHE SAT THERE WAITING FOR THE TIME TO BOARD THE BUS, THEN ANDREA SMILED SOMEONE ELSE LOVES AND CARES ABOUT ME BESIDES MY AUNT AND RANDY AT THIS POINT ANDREA WAS HAPPY FOR A FEW HOURS, ANDREA STANDS UP AND WALKS TOWARDS THE WINDOW I THINK I SEE MY BUS COMING, YES IT IS MY BUS SHE RUNS TO GET A DRINK OF WATER AND GRABS HER BAGS AND IS READY FOR THAT LONG TRIP BACK HOME, AS SHE LOOOKED UP SHE SAW THE BUS PULL INTO THE BUS STATION THERE ARE MANY THNNGS IN MY LIFE THAT HAPPEN THAT I WILL NEVER BE ABLE TO CHANGE, BUT I TURN THE BAD INTO SOMETHING GOOD LIFE IS HARD AND ONE MUST NEVER GIVE UP DON'T MATTER HOW HARD IT GETS. THE THINGS IN MY LIFE THAT I CAN NOT CHANGE I WILL USE THEM AS MY WAY TO MAKE THINGS BETTER IN MY LIFE, AND THE THINGS I CAN CHANGE I WILL USE THAT AS A HEALING PROCESS FOR MY HEART TO MAKE ME STRONGER FOR WHAT I AM GOING TO FACE WHEN I GET BACK HOME. I KNOW IT IS GOING TO BE A BATTLE AND LOT'S OF TEARS AND PAIN ARE GOING TO HAPPEN BUT I WILL ACCOMPLISH WHAT I HAVE TO DO THIS IS A PROMISE I AM MAKING MYSELF. I WONDER HOW THINGS WOULD HAVE TURNED OUT IF I WOULD HAVE NEVER CAME AND STAYED WITH MY AUNT AND GRANDMA, I WOULD OF NOT FOUND OUT THE TRUTH ABOUT MY PARENTS THE TRUE EVIL PEOPLE THEY ARE I DID NOT KNOW MY OLDER SISTER WAS MY MOM, AND MY BROTHER WAS BORN WHEN MY MOM WAS ONLY 17 YEARS OLD MY PARENTS ARE SO

CHAPTER 4   MY HOMETOWN

TWISTED, AS I START WAKING OUT THE DOOR TO BOARD THE BUS I GRAB MY SUIT CASE AND TICKET AS I GO TO THE DOOR I STOP FOR A MOMENT AND JUST SMILE THEN AS I AM WALKING OUT OF THE DOOR I SEE A DISTURBING NEWS ON TV OF HOW A BOY MY AGE WAS RAN OVER BY A CAR THEY HAVE NO SUSPECTS AT THIS PRESENT MOMENT AND THEY DO NOT KNOW WHO THE BOY IS, I PRAY HE IS DOING GOOD PRAYERS GO OUT TO HIM AND HIS FAMILY WAIT NO IT CAN NOT BE BUT WHAT IF IT IS RANDY, NO IT IS NOT HIM HE IS AT HIS HOME WAITING FOR ME TO COME BACK HOME TO HIM BUT WHAT IF IT IS HIM I WOULD LOSE IT, HE PROMISE HE WOULD NEVER LEAVE ME I KNOW WHEN I GET BACK I AM GOING STRAIGHT TO HIS HOUSE. AND WHEN I SEE HIM, I AM GOING TO GIVE HIM THE BIGGEST KISS AND HUG AS WE TAKE OFF, I AM EXCITED AS WE GET ON THE ROAD, I SEE ALL THE SITES I SAW ON MY WAY TO MY GRANDMA HOUSE I STARTED THINKING OF HOW I WAS HEART BROKEN, AS I GOT THERE I SAW LOTS OF LOVE AND HAPPINESS, IN THERE EYES I NEEDED TO FIND MYSELF AND COME BACK WITH A HAPPY HEART AND BE THE WONDERFUL PERSON I INTENDED TO BE, BEFORE ALL OF THIS ABUSE STARTED A FEW YEARS AGO, WE ARE PASSING THE CURVE WHERE I SAID I WISH I COULD DISAPPEAR INTO THOSE MONTAINS, HIDE IN THOSE TREES NOW AS I SEE THEM I SAY I AM BLESSED TO BE PASSNG THESE BEAUTIFUL MOUNTAINS AND TREES. A FEW MORE HOURS AND I WILL BE BACK HOME I WILL CLOSE MY EYES AND THINK ABOUT EVERYTHING AND HOPEFULLY WHEN I OPEN THEM, I WILL BE IN ROSENBERG, AS ANDREA CLOSE HER EYES AND THINKS ABOUT EVERYTHING THAT SHE HAS TO DO WHEN SHE GET'S HOME, AFTER EVERYTHING THAT HAPPEN TO HER, SHE IS HAPPY SHE IS GOING HOME BUT LITTLE DOES SHE KNOW THAT HER BOYFRIEND RANDY. WHICH IS IN THE HOSPITAL STILL IN A COMA AND HAS BEEN FOR THE PASS 2 WEEKS. HER PARENTS ARE STILL UP TO NO GOOD DRINKING AND DOING DRUGS AND NOW THEY HAVE A YOUNG GIRL STAYING WITH THEM, SHE IS ONLY 13 YEARS OLD BUT THIS GIRL IS NOT A FAMILY MEMBER THEY KIDNAP HER FROM

THE PARK. THEY ARE DOING THE SAME TO HER AS THEY DID TO ANDREA, THE BUS HAS ARRIVED AT ROSENBERG LET'S SEE WHAT HAPPENS NEXT WHEN ANDREA GET'S OFF THE BUS, AND SURPRISE HER PARENTS WITH THE COPS AND HOW SHE WILL FEEL WHEN SHE FINDS OUT RANDY IS IN THE HOSPITAL. I AM FINALLY HOME FIRST THING I NEED TO DO IS GO TO THE COPS, BUT I ALSO NEED TO GO SEE RANDY I KNOW HE IS GOING TO BE SURPRISED TO SEE ME AS I GRAB MY BAGS, I SEE MY OLD FRIEND LOOKING AT ME WITH THE SADDEST EYES WHAT IS WRONG JUDY NOTHING ANDREA I WILL TELL YOU LATER, HOW CAN YOU SAY NOTHING YOU CALLED ME WHEN I WAS IN AUSTIN TEXAS SAID YOU HAD SOMETHING IMPORTANT TO TELL ME, NOW WHAT IS IT IS OK ANDREA GO DO WHAT YOU HAVE TO DO AND COME TO MY HOUSE LATER TODAY. PLEASE DON'T FORGET AND COME OVER I DO NOT CARE WHAT TIME IT IS JUST BE AT MY HOUSE OK JUDY TALK TO YOU LATER, AS I WALKED AWAY, I WAS SO CONFUSED I DID NOT KNOW WHAT TO THINK IT DISTURB ME THAT SHE COULD NOT TELL ME WHAT SHE NEEDED TO TELL ME, I WONDER IF IT HAD ANYTHING TO DO WITH THE ACCIDENT I HEARD ON TV I GUESS I WILL FIND OUT SOON ENOUGH, AS I AM WALKING TO THE POLICE STATION I COULD NOT HELP BUT TO THINK ABOUT ALL THE ABUSED IT PLAYS OVER AND OVER IN MY HEAD, THE SAD PART I SUFFERED IN THE HANDS OF MY PARENTS A CHILD IS SUPPOSED TO FEEL SAFE AND LOVED AND TAKEN CARE OF BY THEIR PARENTS, NOT ABUSE AND TREATED LIKE A DOG THE WAY THEY TREATED ME WAS A NIGHTMARE AND TO STAND THEIR AND LAUGH AT ME, WHILE I WAS GETTING ABUSED BY THESE GROWN MAN IT IS MORE THAN A 12 YEAR OLD GIRL SHOULD GO THREW, I THANK GOD HE GAVE ME THE STRENGTH TO OVERCOME ALL I HAVE BEEN PUT THREW NOW TODAY IS THE DAY THAT I WILL GET JUSTICE, FOR WHAT THEY DID TO ME I WILL BE THE ONE LAUGHING AT THE END THEY WILL FINALLY SEE WHAT IF FEEELS LIKE TO BE IN THE HANDS OF OTHER PEOPLE. AND TO SUFFER IN THEIR HANDS AS I STAND OUTSIDE OF THE POLICE STATION, I AM KINDA NERVOUS. I PAUSED AT THE DOOR AND EVERY STEP I TAKE MAKES ME KINDA SCARED, WHAT IF THEY DON'T BELIEVE ME WHAT IF THEY THINK I AM MAKING ALL OF THIS UP. I HAVE TO GO IN AND REPORT THEM AS I GET TO THE FRONT DESK I AM GREETED BY THE POLICEMAN; HOW CAN I HELP YOU; I STAYED QUIET HE ASKED ME AGAIN MAMA HOW CAN WE HELP YOU, I OPENED UP I,I,I, WANT TO REPORT ABUSE AND THEN I BUSTED OUT CRYING THE COP CAME FROM BEHIND THE DESK GAVE ME A TISSUE, COME WITH ME LET'S GO TALK TO THE DETECTIVE AS WE WALKED INTO THE ROOM I SEE TWO DETECTIVES SITTING AT THEIR DESK, THEY ASK THE COP WHAT IS GOING ON WITH A SURPRISED LOOK ON HIS FACE, HE RESPONDED SHE WANTS TO REPORT CHILD ABUSE BY HER PARENTS, THEY LOOKED PUZZLE

AND THEN ONE OF THE DETECTIVES GRAB A CHAIR AND PLACED IT NEXT TO HER DESK, COME HERE AND SIT DOWN WHAT IS YOUR NAME. I AM ANDREA GARCIA. HI MY NAME IS DETECTIVE MARTINEZ AND THIS IS DETECTIVE REYES. WE ARE HERE TOI HELP YOU NOW TELL US WHAT HAPPEN I STAYED QUITE FOR A MOMENT EMBARRASSED OF WHAT I WAS GOING TO TELL THEM, ANDREA TELL US WHAT HAPPEN SO WE CAN HELP YOU MY PARENTS WERE NOT GOOD PARENTS THEY DRANK ALOT AND WOULD ALWAYS HIT ME, NOW ANDREA YOU CAN NOT FILE CHARGES ON YOUR PARENTS FOR HITTING YOU I NEW THIS WAS A MISTAKE AS I GET UP TO LEAVE THE DETECTIVE GOT UP AND STOP ME, MR REYES LET HER FINISH DO NOT ASSUME UNTIL YOU GET THE WHOLE STORY, CONTINUE ANDREA AS I WAS SAYING MY PARENTS WERE NOT SUCH GOOD PARENTS THEY ABUSE ME AT FIRST I THOUGHT THEY WERE HITTING ME CAUSE I WAS DOING SOMETHING WRONG. WHEN DID THE ABUSE START IT STARTED WHEN I WAS 9 YEARS OLD, I AM 16 NOW I AM NOT REPORTING THEM FOR HITTING ME I AM REPORTING THEM FOR WHAT MY DAD DID TO ME AND MY MOM WOULD LET HIM AND LAUGH AT ME, WHAT DID YOUR DAD DO TO YOU I LOOKED DOWN ANDREA WHAT DID YOUR DAD DO TO YOU, MY DAD WOULD COME INTO MY ROOM AT NIGHT AND DO THINGS TO ME HE TOOK ADVANTAGE OF ME HE TOOK MY INNOCENCE.HE WOULD SALE ME TO HIS FRIENDS TO BUY HIS DRUGS I COULD NOT BELIEVE THIS WAS HAPPENING TO ME SO I DO NOT EXPECT YOU TO BELIEVE IT NITHER, HE DID ALL OF THIS FOR HIS DRUGS AND PLEASURE THE DETECTIVE WAS SHOCKED WHEN I TOLD HER THIS AND SHE ASKED ME DO YOU HAVE PROOF, YES I DO I REMEMBER I WAS IN LOT'S OF PAIN I COULD NOT EVEN WALK AFTER I WAS ABUSE THAT NIGHT BY 3 MEN, AS I WAS THERE AT THE HOSPITAL THEY NOTICED THE ABUSE THEY CALLED THE COPS AND THE COPS MADE A REPORT OF WHAT THEY FOUND, THE DETECTIVE LOOKED AT THE POLICE REPORT FROM THAT NIGHT AS SHE READ IT TEARS WERE FALLING FROM HER EYES, AS SHE LOOKED AT ME SHE SAID OH MY GOD I AM SO SORRY THIS HAPPEN TO YOU, I STARTED CRYING I BEG THEM TO STOP THAT THEY WERE HURTING ME MY DAD SAID GOOD GIRL MAKE DADDY HAPPY, AND THEY LAUGH AT ME WHY DID THEY DO THIS TO ME WHY DON'T THEY LOVE ME I NEVER DID NO WRONG I WAS A GOOD DAUGHTER, AFTER I GAVE MY REPORT THEY SENT THE COPS TO MY PARENTS HOUSE AND HAD THEM ARRESTED BOTH MY DAD FRIENDS WERE NEVER FOUND. MY PARENTS WERE CHARGE WITH CHILD ABUSE AND ASSAULT CAUSING INJURY TO A CHILD, ENDANGERMENT TO A CHILD THAT DAY MY PARENTS GOT ARRESTED AS I WAS LEAVING THE POLICE STATION, THE DETECTIVE SAID YOU ARE A VERY BRAVE AND STRONG YOUND LADY TO COME FORWARD LIKE THIS AGAINST YOUR PARENTS. AS I WAS LEAVING THE STATION I

SAW THE COPS BRINGING MY PARENTS IN THAT WAS THE HAPPIEST DAY OF MY LIFE, NOW THAT I AM DONE HERE, I CAN GO SEE RANDY AND GIVE HIM THE GOOD NEWS ON MY WAY TO HIS HOUSE I SEE HIS OLD FRIEND HIS BEST FRIEND TIM, COMING UP THE ROAD I HAVE NOT SEEN HIM IN YEARS HE NOTICE ME, WALKING UP TOWARDS HIM AS HE STOP HE JUST LOOK AT ME FOR A BIT NOT SAYING A WORD. IN A LOW VOICE HE ASK SO HOW IS RANDY DOING? HEY TIM, I DON'T KNOW I AM GOING TO HIS HOUSE RIGHT NOW OH MY GOD SO YOU DON'T KNOW WHAT HAPPENED TO HIM WHILE YOU WERE GONE. WHAT YOU MEAN TELL ME COME ON GET IN I WILL TELL YOU ON THE WAY TO THE HOSPITAL WHEN HE SAID THAT MY HEART JUST DROPPED, I JUMPED I TEH CAR AS FAST AS I COULD OK NOW TELL ME WHAT HAPPEN OK DID YOU HEAR THE NEWS ON TV ABOUT THE BOY THAT WAS RAN OVER, WHEN HE SAID THIS I SCREAMED OUT AS LOUD AS I COULD SAYING NO IT CAN NOT BE TRUE, NOT MY RANDY THIS IS A LIE HE CANNOT BE IN THE HOSPITAL TELL ME YOU ARE PLAYING WITH ME. AS I SIT THERE SOBBING FULL OF TEARS IN A LOW VOICE HE PROMISED HE WOULD NEVER LEAVE ME STOP PLAHING WHERE IS HE FOR REAL, PLEASE SAY THIS IS NOT TRUE PLEASE I CAN NOT LOSE HIM I LOVE HIM SO MUCH AND HE PROMISED ME WE SOULD ALWAYS BE TOGETHER, OK TIM IKNOW HE IS DOING THIS TO PAY ME BACK FOR BEING GONE ALL THESE MONTHS AND NOT TALKING TO HIM, I LEARNED MY LESSON NOW TAKE ME BACK TO HIS HOUSE THIS IS NOT FUNNY. ANDREA I AM SO SORRY THIS IS NOT A GAME I AM SO SERIOUS AS HE IS LOOKING AT ME WITH TEARS IN HIS EYES, I AM TELLING YOU THE TRUTH. HE IS HERE IN THE HOSPITAL AS WE GOIT TO THE HOSPITAL I DID NOT EVEN LET THE CAR STOP COMPLETELY, I JUMPED OUT AND RAN INSIDE THE HOSPITAL ASKING THE LADY AT THE FRONT WHAT ROOM IS RANDY GARCIA IN. HE IS IN ROOM 223 ON THE SECOND FLOOR BUT MAMA RANDY IS STILL IN A COMA AS SHE SAID I DROP TO MY KNEES CRYING AND PRAYING THAT HE GET'S BETTER, I JUMP UP RAN TO HIS ROOM I HAVE TO BE STRONG FOR HIM AS I GOT TO THE SECOND FLOOR I SLOWLY WALKED TO HIS ROOM, I COULDL NOT BELIEVE WHAT I WAS LOOKING AT IT WAS LIKE I WAS IN A BAD DREAM. AS TEARS WERE FALLING FROM MY EYES, I SLOWLY OPEN THE DOOR AS I WALKED IN, I COULD NOT BELIEVE WHAT I WAS LOOKING AT AS HE WAS LAYING THERE WITH TUBES ALL OVER HIS BODY, I WENT UP TO HIM STANDING BY HIS BEDSIDE I HELD HIS HAND AS I SPOKE TO HIM I AM HERE RANDY I MADE IT BACK AS I PROMISE SEE I PROMISE YOU I WOULD NEVER LEAVE YOU. AND REMEMBER YOU PROMISE ME YOU WOULD NEVER LEAVE ME I AM HERE FOR YOU AND I WILL BE BY YOUR SIDE UNTIL YOU ARE READY TO GO HOME, I WAITED MANY MONTHS TO SEE YOU AS I WAS TALKING TO HIM, I WAS REMEMBERING THE FIRST TIME THAT WE MEET AND

ALL THE GOOD TIMES WE SPENT TOGETHER THOSES LATE NIGHT WALKS IN THE PARK ALL THE LETTERS HE WROTE ME, THEN I SAID TO HIME LOOK RANDY I STILL HAVE THE FIRST LETTER YOU WROTE ME LET ME READ IT TO YOU. YOU WROTE; DEAR ANDREA I AM SO HAPPY I MET YOU THANK YOU FOR COMING INTO MY LIFE THAT DAY I MET YOU WAS THE HAPPIEST DAY OF MY LIFE, AND I PROMISE YOU I WILL DO MY BEST TO MAKE EVERY DAY YOUR HAPPIEST DAY. I WILL NEVER LEAVE YOU OR HURT I AM HERE FOR YOU. I PLAN ON GETTING MARRIED TO YOU ONE OF THESE DAY'S WILL GOTTA GO TO CLASS TELL I SEE YOU LATER LOVE YOU MY FUTURE WIFE; SEE RANDY THE PROMISE YOU MADE ME AS I WAS TELLING RANDY THIS, I SAW TEARS COMING FROM HIS EYES PLEASE WAKE UP DON'T LEAVE ME I NEED YOU AS I SAW HE WAS RESPONDING TO ME THAT WAS A RELIFE IN MY HEART. AS I WAS TALKING TO HIM, I SAW TIM STANDING IN THE DOORWAY WITH TEARS IN HIS EYES TIM IT IS OK HE IS JUST RESTING, HE WILL WAKE UP SOON TIM STAYED WITH US AT THE HOSPITAL FOR A FEW DAYS, HE HAD TO GO BACK HOME AS HE WAS LEAVING HE SAID I WILL BE BACK IN A FEW DAYS. TELL RANDY I WAS HERE I WILL BE BACK AND DON'T FORGET TO LOOK UP INTO THE SKY FOR THERE HE WILL FIND HIS HAPPINESS AND STRENGHT HE NEEDS TO MAKE OUT OF THIS, AS TIM WALK AWAY, I HEARD HIM PRAY TO GOD AS HE PRAYED, HE ASK GOD TO PLEASE HELP RANDY OUT OF THIS TRAUMA HE IS IN YOUR MERCIFUL HANDS I LEAVE HIS LIFE IN YOUR HANDS AMEN. AS HE WAS PRAYING, I STOOD THERE WITH TEARS IN MY *EYES* PRAYING THAT GOD ANSWER HIS PRAYERS AS TIM LEFT, I JUST STOOD THERE IN A DAZE AS I CAME OUT OF MY DAZE BY THE MOST WONDERFUL VOICE I EVER HEARD, I LOOKED AT RANDY HE HAD FINALLY OPENED HIS EYES THE FIRST WORDS HE SAID ANDREA ARE YOU HERE, AS I HELD HIS HAND I SAID YES MY LOVE I AM HEREE FOR YOU TRY NOT TO TALK GET YOUR REST, I PROMISE YOU I WILL NEVER LEAVE YOU AND I WILL BE BY YOUR SIDE WHE WHOLE TIME, YOU ARE HERE IN THIS HOSPITAL WHEN YOU GO HOME I WILL BE BY YOUR SIDE THE WHOLE TIME TO TAKE CARE OF YOU. I MISS YOU SO MUCH HE LOOKED AT ME WITH TEARS IN HIS EYES AND I ASKED HIM WHAT HAPPEN MY LOVE, I ALMOST LOST MY LIFE IN THIS ACCIDENT BUT I KNEW I COULD NOT LEAVE YOU I FOUGHT TO STAY ALIVE FOR YOU, MY LOVE. LOOK ANDREA THERE IS SOMETHING I HAVE TO TELL YOU WILL THIS WAS NOT AN ACCIDENT WHAT DO YOU MEAN IT WAS NOT AN ACCIEDNT, YES DO YOU REMEMBER YOUR EX-BOYFRIEND JIMMY YES WHAT ABOUT HIM WILL HE IS THE ONE THAT RAN ME OVER AS I WAS LAYING ON THE GROUND HE SAID IF I CAN NT HAVE ANDREA NOBODY CAN THEN HE JUST WALKED AWAY, HE TRIED TO KILL ME BUT HE DID NOT SUCCEED I KNOW WHEN HE FINDS OUT I AM STILL ALIVE HE IS GOING TO TRY AGAIN, DON'T WORRY WE ARE GOING TO CALL THE COPS ON

HIM AND HAVE HIM ARRESTED, AS I HAD MY PARENTS ARRESTED AS I SAID THIS RANDY LOOKED AT ME WHEN I SAID THIS YOU HAD YOUR PARENTS ARRESTED, WHEN DID THIS HAPPEN I STOP BY THE POLICE STATION ON MY HERE AND FILEDS CHARGES ON THEM AND NOW THEY ARE IN JAIL, FOR EVERYTHING THEY DID TO ME SINCE I WAS 9 YEARS OLD RANDY I WAS ONLY 9 AND THEY DESTROYED MY LIFE, BUT NOW THEY WILL GET WHAT THEY HAVE COMING TO THEM MAY THEIR SOUL BE IN GODS HANDS, AS I FINISHED TELLING RANDY THIS HE WAS SPEECHLESS THEN HE LOOKED AT ME LOOK ANDREA I HAVE SOMETHING TO TELL YOU NOW THE DAY WHEN WE FIRST GOT TOGETHER, I NEVER KNEW OUR LOVE WOULD GROW AS STRONG AS IT HAS AND I THANK GOD FOR YOU MY LOVE, WE HAD BEEN THREW ALOT TOGETHER THERE WERE TIMES WHEN IT HAS COME TO THE POINT IN OUR LIVES THAT IT DOES NOT MATTER WHAT PEOPLE SAY. TO TRY AND KEEP US APART THE MORE THEY TRY THE CLOSER WE BECOME THAT DAY YOU BECAME MY GIRLFRIEND JOEL TOLD ME HE WOULD NOT STOP TRYING UNTIL YOU BECAME HIS GIRLFRIEND, BUT I KNEW YOU WOULD NOT BE HAPPY WITH HIM BECAUSE WE BELONG TOGETHER AND ONE DAY YOU WILL BE MY WIFE. WHEN I HEARD THOSE WORDS, MY HEART JUST STOP, I WAS SO FULL OF JOY AND HAPPINESS THEN I THOUGHT THAT THEIR WAS ONE PERSON IN MY LIFE THAT WOULD WANT TO SPEND THE REST OF THEIR LIFE WITH ME THIS IS A BLESSING, THAT SOUNDS GREAT RANDY NOW THE FIRST THING WE MUST DO IS GET YOU OUT OF HERE I LOVE YOU RANDY I LOVE YOU ANDREA AND I THANK GOD EVERY DAY THAT I HAVE YOU IN MY LIFE, AS RANDY SAID THIS A HAPPY TEAR CAME FROM MY EYES I WILL BE RIGHT BACK RANDY LET ME GO TALK TO THE DR AND SEE WHAT THE NEXT STEP IS TO GET YOU OUT OF HERE, AS I GET UP TO GO LOOK FOR THE DR. I AM HOPING TO HEAR SOME GOOD NEWS EXCUSE ME DR, YES MAY I HELP YOU I CLEAR MY THROAT YES HOW MUCH LONGER IS RANDY GARCIA GOING TO BE HERE IN THE HOSPITAL. WILL MRS. HAD SUFFER A BAD ACCIDENT HE WILL HAVE TO STAY HERE FOR THERAPY NOW THE THERAPY WILL LAST 1 OR 2 WEEKS, DEPENDING ON HOW RANDY RESPONDS TO THE TREATMENT SO WHAT IS YOUR RELATIONSHIP TO HIM. I SMILED HE IS MY FIANCE OK MRS. GARCIA LET'S GET YOUR FUTURE HUSBAND BETTER AND YOU BOTH CAN GO HOME SOON, THAT SOUNDS GREAT DR. RANDY WILL BE HAPPY TO HEAR THIS WE ENTER THE ROOM I HAVE A SMILE ON MY FACE, RANDY LOOKED AT ME WHAT HAPPEN TELL ME WILL MY LOVE THE DR. SAID YOU HAVE TO DO SOME THERAPY AND THEN YOU CAN GO HOME, NOW ANDREA I NEED YOU TO STAND BY RANDY SIDE AND SUPPORT HIM DURING HIS TREATMENT, YES DR. I WILL DO WHATEVER I NEED TO DO SO RANDY CAN GET BETTER AS I WAS TALKING TO THE DR., WE SAW RANDY TRYING

TO GET OUT OF BED WHERE ARE YOIU TRYING TO GO I AM READY TO START MY TREATMENT SO I CAN GO HOME, YOUR THERAPY WILL START TOMORROW ANDREA STANDS BY RANDY HAND AS SHE LOOKS INTO HIS EYES I LOVE YOU AND YOU ARE VERY SPECIAL TO ME I LOVE YOU TO ANDREA, THE DR. WAS STANDING THERE THEN HE SAID THAT IS SO SPECIAL I SEE YOU BOTH HAVE A SPECIAL LOVE FOR ONE ANOTHER I HARDLY SEE THAT KIND OF LOVE. WILL RANDY GET YOUR REST SEE YOU IN THE MORNING, AS THE DR. STANDS AT THE DOOR OF THE ROOM HE OVERHEARS ANDREA AND RANDY PRAY LORD WE COME TO YOU IN PRAYER LAYING OUR PETITION AT YOUR FEET, TO PLEASE HELP RANDY GET WILL YOU SEE THE PAIN AND SUFFERING HE HAS BEEN GOING THREW WE LEAVE HIS HEALTH IN YOUR MERCIFUL HANDS AMEN, AS RANDY AND ANDREA SAID THEIR PRAYER THE DR. ALSO WAS PRAYING AS RANDY AND ANDREA LOOKED AT THE DR. AT THE SAME TIME THEY BOTH SAID THANK YOU. FOR ALL YOU HAVE DONE FOR RANDY THE DR. JUST SMILE AND LEAVES THE ROOM, YOU KNOW ANDREA THERE IS MUCH WE CAN BE THANKFUL FOR IN OUR LIVES BUT THE ONLY THING THAT I AM MOST THANKFUL IS HAVING A WONDERFUL PARTNER BY MY SIDE, MY LOVE YOU HAVE BEEN THEIR FOR ME WHEN I NEEEDED YOU THE MOST WHEN EVER ONE ELSE FAILED ME YOU WERE THERE, NOT GIVING UP ON ME AS IF YOU KNEW IN YOUR HEART THE I WOULD COME OUT ON TOP AND FOR THAT I SAY THANK YOU I LOVE YOU. YOUR WELCOME RANDY I ENJOY AND LOVE EVERY MOMENT THAT WE HAVE BEEN TOGETHER AND I DO NOT REGREAT ANYTHING WHEN IT COMES TO YOU OUR LOVE IS A LOVE MADE IN HEAVEN, I GIVE GOD ALL THE THANKS FOR BRINGING US TOGETHER AS ANDREA AND RANDY STOP TALKING, THEY STAYED THERE SILENT NOT SAYING A WORD ALL THEY COULD DO WAS THINK ABOUT THE FOLLOWING DAY WHICH WAS GOING TO BE A BIG DAY, WHICH WOULD BE THE FIRST DAY OF RANDY TREATMENT THEY BOTH WAITED AND HOPE FOR THIS DAY TO COME, WHERE RANDY WOULD GET THE TREATMENT HE NEEDED TO BE ABLE TO WALK AGAIN.

CHAPTER 5   THE RECOVERY

AND FULLY RECOVER FROM THE ACCIDENT THAT HE WENT THREW NOW WE WILL SEE HOW THAT FIRST DAY TURNS OUT, ANDREA THERE IS SOMETHING I NEED TO TELL YOU WHAT IS IT RANDY ALOT HAS HAPPENED IN MY LIFE BUT I PROMISE YOU WHEN I GET OUT OF THIS HOSPITAL, I WILL DO Y BEST TO MAKE YOU THE HAPPIEST PERSON IN THE WORLD AS ANDREA LOOKED AT ME RANDY DO YOU REALLY PROMISE WHAT YOU JUST SAID? YES, I PROMISE WHEN I WENT TO STAY AT MY AUNT AND GRANDMA HOUSE FOR THOSES FEW MONTHS THEY SHOWED ME MORE LOVE AND COMPASSION THEN MY PARENTS DID ALL MY LIFE, I COULD NOT IMAGINE THAT IT WOULD BE SO WONDERFUL STAYING WITH THEM. WILL THAT IS GREAT ANDREA I AM HAPPY FOR YOU WILL RANDY, I TOLD THEM WHEN I WAS DONE HER AND ACCOMPLISH WHAT I NEEDED TO I WOULD RETURN AND GO LIVE WITH THEM, WHEN I SAID THIS RANDY STARTED CRYING SO YOU ARE LEAVING ME FOR GOOD NO WAIT, I AM NOT FINISHED TELLING YOU SO WHAT ELSE HAPPEND ASKING ME THIS AS HE WAS LOOKING AT ME WITH THE SADDEST EYES WAS BRINGING TEARS TO MY EYES, MY LOVE I TOLD GRANDMA WHEN I GO BACK TO STAY WITH THEM I WAS GOING TO TAKE YOU WITH ME AND SHE SAID SHE WOULD LOVE TO MEET YOU, WHEN I SAID THIS I SAW THE LOOK OF HAPPINESS ON RANDY'S FACE GREAT ANDREA I WOULD LOVE TO GO BACK WITH YOU AND MEET YOUR GRANDMA AND AUNT AND WHERE EVER YOU GO I GO AFTER ALL YOU ARE MY FURTURE WIFE, YES RANDY AND YOU ARE MY FUTURE HUSBAND. I WAS PLEASE AND RELIEVED KNOWING THAT WE WILL BE TOGETHER FOREVER, OK RANDY IT IS GETTING LATE IT IS TIME WE GET SOME REST I WILL SLEEP ON THE COUCH I AM HERE FOR YOU, IF YOU NEED ANYTHING MY LOVE, I HAVE EVERYTHING I NEED AS WE GAVE EACH OTHER OUR GOODNIGHT KISS WE BOTH FAIL INTO A DEEP SLEEP. AS THEY BOTH SLEPT THAT NIGHT ALL THEY COULD DO WAS DREAM ABOUT THEIR LIVES TOGETHER, AND SOON MORNING WILL BE HERE AND THEN EVERYTHING THEY BEEN PRAYING FOR COME TO PASS, AND THE START OF A NEW LIFE WITH NEW HOPES AND

DREAMS WILL SOON HAPPEN THEY BOTH SUFFER SO MUCH IN THERE LIVES NOW IT IS TIME FOR HEALING AND RECOVERY TO BEGIN. GOOD MORNING RANDY GOOD MORNING ANDREA HOW WAS YOUR NIGHT WITH A SMILE ON HER FACE IT WAS THE BEST NIGHT EVER, HOW WAS YOUR NIGHT I STAYED SILENT AS I THOUGHT ABOUT IT MY LOVE IT WAS A BLESSING I LAID HERE IN THIS BED MANY NIGHTS AND COULD NOT SLEEP DON'T MATTER HOW HARD I TRIED I COULD NOT SLEEP AND I COULD NOT WAKE UP, BUT WITH YOU HERE IT HAS MADE MY LIFE A WHOLE LOT BETTER I LOVE YOU ANDREA YOU ARE THE BEST. AND THANKS TO YOU IT IS A BLESSING TO BE ABLE TO WAKE UP AFTER A GOOD NIGHT RESST, WILL RANDY THEY WILL BE HERE SOON TO START YOUR THERAPY. ANDREA I AM A LITTLE NERVOUS WHAT IF I FALL DOWN WHEN I TRY TO GET UP MY LOVE DON'T WORRY, I AM HERE WITH YOU AND I WON'T LET YOU FALL OR HURT YOUR SELF AS ANDREA SAID THIS THE DOOR TO THE ROOM SLOWLY OPEN IT WAS THE DR. GOOD MORNING DR. WE ARE READY TO GO, WILL RANDY FIRST WE ARE GOING TO START HERE IN THE ROOM DR. WHAT KIND OF THERAPY CAN WE DO HERE IN THE ROOM FIRST I NEED TO SEE IF YOU CAN STAND UP ON YOUR OWN RANDY STARTED PULLING THE SHEETS OFF HIM, AS THE DR WAS SPEAKING TO HIM HOLD ON MR. GARCIA LET'S TAKE IT NICE AND SLOW I AM READY OK RANDY GRAB MY ARM AND PULL YOURSELF UP, AS RANDY WAS TRYING I WAS TELLING RANDY COME ON YOU CAN DO IT I BELIEVE IN YOU SHOW US HOW MUCH YOU WANT THIS, IT IS UP TO YOU RANDY HOW LONG YOUR THERAPY WILL LAST AS I SAID THIS RANDY PULLED HIMSELF ALL THE WAY UP I AM SO PROUD OF YOU I KNEW YOU COULD DO IT. THE DR ASKED RANDY SO HOW ARE YOU FEELING IS THERE ANY PAIN ANYWHERE IN YOUR BODY NO DR. I FEEL NO PAIN IN MY BODY THAT IS GREAT I AM GETTING A BED LIFT ROPE AND YOU WILL BE DOING BED LIFTS EXERCISES EVERY MORNING, AS PART OF YOUR TREATMENT WHICH WILL START IN THE MORNING, I WILL HAVE THE NURSE COME GET YOU AFTER BREAKFAST TO START YOUR REHABILITATION, OK DR. THAT SOUNDS GREAT AS THE DOCTOR WALK OUT OF THE ROOM RANDY LOOKED AT ANDREA IT FELT GREAT I DID NOT FEEL ANY PAIN, I HOPE THE REST OF THE THERAPY GOES AS SMOOTHLY AS THIS DID, YES MY LOVE I KNOW YOU ARE A VERY STRONG PERSON AND YOU HAVE THE WILL POWER TO WANT TO GET BETTER. THAT IS A GREAT SIGN AND I ASSURE YOU THAT YOU WILL GET DONE WITH YOUR THERAPY SOONER THAN YOU THINK, AS ANDREA WAS SPEAKING TO RANDY, SHE HEARD HER NAME CALLED OUT ON THE INTERCOM RANDY AND ANDREA LOOKED AT EACH OTHER PUZZLE AS WHO COULD BE CALLING HER HERE AT THE HOSPITAL. AS ANDREA GOES AND SEE WHO IS CALLING HER SHE IS THINKING WHO CAN IT BE NO ONE KNOWS I AM HERE

WITH RANDY, AS SHE GET'S TO THE DESK SHE SPEAKS I AM ANDREA THERE WAS A CALL FOR ME? AS THEY HAND ME THE PHONE, I HEAR ALOT OF BACKGROUND NOISE HELLO THIS IS ANDREA WHO IS CALLING ME? HELLO, ANDREA IM DETECTIVE MARTINEZ REMEMBER WE TALKED A FEW WEEKS AGO AT THE STATION, YES HOW IS EVERYTHING GOING DETECTIVE MARTINEZ WILL ANDREA THAT IS THE REASON I CALLED, ARE YOU READY TO GO TO COURT AND TESTIFY AGAINST YOUR PARENTS THE TRIAL STARTS NEXT WEEK AND WE ARE GOING TO NEED YOU THERE TO SPEAK ON YOUR BEHALF, NOW ANDREA IT IS GOING TO BE THE HARDEST THING YOU WILL HAVE TO DO YOUR WHOLE LIFE NO THAT IS NOT THE HARDEST THING I WOULD HAVE TO DO MY WHOLE LIFE, YOU KNOW WHAT WAS THE HADREST THING I HAVE TO DO MY WHOLE LIFE THAT WAS STAYING IN THE SAME HOUSE WITH TWO MONSTERS, AND GETTING ABUSED EVERYDAY OF YOUR LIFE AND YOUR DAD COMES INTO YOUR ROOM AT NIGHT AND HAS HIS WAY WITH YOU AND IT DOES NT MATTER HOW MUCH YOU CRY AND BEG HIM TO STOP HE WOULD NOT. HE WOULD JUST LAUGH AND DID OT GET OFF OF YOU AND YOUR MOM IN THE NEXT ROOM LAUGHING AT YOUR PAIN THE WHOLE TIME, WHICH IS THE HARDEST THING ONE WOULD HAVE TO DO IN THEIR WHOLE LIFE SO THIS IS A PICE OF CAKE AFTER I TOLD THE DETECTIVE THIS SHE STAYED SILENT FOR A BIT I COULD HEAR HER CRYING AND I SAID IT WILL BE OK AND I WILL BE THERE NEXT WEEK, AFTER WE HUNG UP I STAYED THERE AT THE DESK WITH MY HAND ON THE PHONE STILL, AND THE NURSE THERE OVER HEARD MY CONVERSATION WITH THE DETECTIVE I SAW TEARS IN HER EYES, SHE SAID MY POOR CHILD NO ONE SHOULD HAVE TO HAVE GONE THREW WHAT YOU EXPERIANCE. I AM GLAD YOU'RE STANDING UP FOR YOURSELF TO SEEK JUSTICE ON YOUR PARENTS OR AS YOU CALL THEM THOSES MONSTERS THANK YOU FOR THOSES KIND WORDS, AS I GO BACK TO RANDY ROOM, I AM FULL OF ALL KINDS OF EMOTIONS I OPEN HIS DOOR WITH A BIG SMILE ON MY FACE SO WHAT WAS THE PHONE CALL ABOUT I HAVE TO GO TO COURT NEXT WEEK, MY PARENTS TRAIL STARTS NEXT WEEK THAT IS GREAT NEWS THINGS ARE FINALLY FALLING INTO PLACE, YES RANDY THEY ARE BUT FOR NOW WE MUST FOCUS ON YOU GETTING BETTER AS I SAT BY RANDY BED HE REACH OUT AND HOLD MY HAND, YOU KNOW RANDY I AM SCARED I HAVE TO FACE THEM AND TELL THE WHOLE WORLD THE MONSTERS THAT THEY ARE AND ALL THE ABUSED THEY DID TO ME, ANDREA ARE YOU SURE YOU ARE READY FOR THIS YES I AM READY NOW YOU KNOW IT IS GOING TO BE ROUGH IN THAT COURTROOM, YES I KNOW BUT THIS IS SOMETHING I HAVE TO DO THEY CAN NOT GET AWAY WITH THIS THEY REALLY DESTROYED MY LIFE. THEY STOLE MY CHILDHOOD THE THNGS THEY TOOK AWAY FROM ME I CAN NEVER GET BACK I AM SUPPOSED TO HAVE A GOOD

MEMORIES, AS A CHILD I AM SUPPOSED TO BE ABLE TO TELL GOOD STORIES OF HOW GREAT MY LIFE WAS AS A CHILD HOW IT WAS GROWING UP. BUT ALL I HAVE IS BAD MEMORIES THAT ARE STILL HUNTING ME, I WAKE UP CRYING AND SCARED FROM THE AWFUL TORTURE MY DAD PUT ME THREW I STILL FEEL ALL THOSES MEN ALL OVER MY BODY, WHEN I SEE SOMEONE COME TO MY DOOR I START CRYING THINKING IT IS MY DAD OR ONE OF THOSES MEN COMING TO HURT ME AGAIN, I CAN STILL HEAR MY DAD VOICE AS HE WOULD COME INTO MY ROOM AT NIGHT'S SAYING IT IS TIME TO PLEASE YOUR DAD AND ALL I COULD DO WAS JUST LAY THERE AND CRY, NO RANDY I AM GOING THREW WITH THIS NOTHING IS GOING TO STOP ME FROM GETTING JUSTICE FOR WHAT I HAVE BEEN THREW, BUT WAIT THIS IS YOUR MOMENT WE NEED TO GET YOU READY FOR YOUR TREATENT. THE NURSE WILL BE HERE SOON TO TAKE YOU TO YOUR FIRST THERAPY AFTER A WHILE THE NURSE CAME TO TAKE RANDY TO HIS TREATMENT, AS THEY WE ARE LEAVING; RANDY LOOK BACK ARE YOU COMING WITH US YES, I AM IF IT IS OK WITH THE NURSE YES, IT IS OK IF YOUR SISTER COMES WITH US. SHE IS NOT MY SISTER, SHE IS MY FIANCE WHEN RANDY SAID THAT I FELT THE LOVE HE HAS FOR ME AS RANDY WAS LOOKING AT ME THE NURSE SMILE OK MRS. GARCIA LET'S GO, AS WE WALKED DOWN THE HALL TO THE THERAPY ROOM, I WAS JUST PRAYING THAT HIS THERAPY WOULD GO GREAT AND WE COULD GO HOME BY THE END OF THE WEK, AS WE GOT TO THE THERAPY HE LOOKED AT ME AND SMILE AND SAID OK MY LOVE THIS IS THE START OF MY RECOVERY. AS RANDY WAS SITTING AT THE CHAIR HE TURN AND LOOKED AT THE NURSE AND SPOKE OK I AM READY FOR THIS AS HE SAID THIS THE THERAPIST WALK IN AND SAID OK MR. GARCIA LET'S START I WANNA SEE HOW STRONG YOUR LEGS ARE TRY TO STAND UP ON MY FIRST ATTEMPT I FAILED BACK DOWN, THE THERAPIST SAID IT IS OK WE JUST HAVE TO WORK AND GET THE STRENGTH BACK IN YOUR LEGS AS I SAT THERE I FELT DEFEATED AS ANDREA AND THE THERAPIST TURNED AROUND TO TALK , I TOOK A DEEP BREATH AND TRIED TO STAND UP AGAIN, AND THIS TIME I ACCOMPLISHED STANDING ON MY OWN TWO FEET WITHOUT HOLDING ONTO ANYTHING AS I WAS STANDING THERE I SAID LOOK MY LOVE THIS THERAPY IS NOT GOING TO BE THAT HARD AFTER ALL. THEY BOTH TURN AROUND AS THEY BOTH SAW ME STANDING ON MY OWN, I SAW TEARS OF JOY IN ANDREA EYES AS THE THERAPIST SPOKE WOW THAT IS AMAZING WITH THAT KIND OF DETERMINATION, I KNOW YOU WILL MAKE GOOD PROGRESS AND YOU WILL BE GOING HOME SOONER THAN YOU THINK. AS THE THERAPIST WAS SPEAKING, I SAW THE LOOK OF RELIFE ON RANDY'S FACE AND I WAS FULL OF JOY I KNOW IT WAS BY THE HEALING HAND OF OUR LORD AND SAVIOR, THAT HE IS GETTING BETTER SO

MUCH FASTER THAN WE HAD IMAGINE RANDY FINISHED HIS THERAPY FOR THAT DAY. ON OUR WAY BACK TO RANDY ROOM WE SAW TIM STANDING AT THE DOORWAY OF RANDY'S ROOM AS WE GOT THEIR HE JUST SMILED TIM WHAT ARE YOU DOING BACK SO SOON, I HAD TO COME BACK TO SEE HOW YOU ARE DOING WE COULD NOT TALK THE LAST TIME I WAS HERE YOU WAS IN A DEEP SLEEP.YES I WAS THANKS FOR COMING AND CHECKING ON ME I JUST FINISH MY FIRST THERAPY THATS GREAT SO HOW DID IT GO, WILL IT WENT GREAT AND THE THERAPIST SAID I COULD GO HOME THIS WEEKEND THAT IS THE BEST NEWS I HEARD IN A LONG TIME. I BEEN WORKING ALOT BUT I TOOK TIME OFF TO COME AND SEE YOU AS TIM SAID THIS, I SAW TEARS COMING OUT OF RANDY EYES ARE OK WHY ARE YOU CRYING I AM GREAT I AM JUST THINKING THAT MY BEST FRIEND TOOK TIME OFF HIS JOB AND LIFE TO COME SPEND TIME WITH ME. JUST AS HE DID BACK IN SCHOOL HE TOOK IT UPON HIM SELF TO MAKE SURE I WAS HAPPY I TELL YOU TIM YOU ARE MORE TO ME THAN JUST A FRIEND YOU ARE MY BROTHER. TIM JUST SMILED AS HE SAID I LOVE YOU MY BROTHER SO HOW ARE THINGS GOING HERE WILL I HAVE GOOD NEWS AND BAD NEWS; I SEE WILL TELL ME THE GOOD NEWS FIRST WILL THE DR. SAID IF I DO GOOD ON MY THERAPY, I COULD GO HOME THIS WEEKEND AND NOW THE BAD NEWS AS I SAID THIS ANDREA PUT HER HEAD DOWN, WHAT IS IT TELL ME WHAT HAPPEND ANDREA TELL HIM WILL TIM THE DETECTIVE CALL ME THE OTHERE DAY HERE, AND TOLD ME THAT NEXT WEEK I HAVE TO APPEAR IN COURT TO TESTIFY AGAINST MY PARENTS, FOR WHAT THEY DID TO ME FOR SO MANY YEARS SO HOW IS THAT BAD NEWS THIS IS WHAT YOU WANTED TO GET JUSTICE FOR WHAT THEY DID TO YOU. WHAT IS THE ISSUE HERE WILL I AM KINDA SCARED TO SEE THEM, LOOK ANDREA THEY WERE NOT SCARED OR HAD NO HEART TO DO TO WHAT THEY DID, YOIU SHOULD NOT BE SCARED TO RETURN THE PAIN THEY IMPOSED ON YOU FOR SO MANY YEARS, AS RANDY GRAB MY HAND HE SAID LOOKED ANDREA YOIU MUST DO THIS DON'T WORRY I WILL BE BY YOUR SIDE THE WHOLE TIME, AND WHEN THIS IS ALL OVER WITH THEN WE CAN CONTINUE WITH THE PLANS THAT WE HAD MADE FOR OUR LIVES. REMEMBER AS YOU PROMISE YOUR AUNT AND GRANDMA, WE WOULD BE GOING BACK TO STAY WITH THEM, WHEN THE TIME IS RIGHT THEN WE WILL SET OUR BIG DAY AND PLAN OUR FUTURE. AS I SPOKE TO ANDREA, SHE STAYED SILENT LOOKING INTO SPACE NOT A WORD TO SAY, I WAS WONDERING WHAT SHE WAS THINKING ANDREA WHAT'S ON YOUR MIND WHY YOU SO QUIET? RANDY FOR YEARS LOT'S HAVE HAPPEN TO THE BOTH OF US. NO ONE WAS THERE TO HELP US OR LISTEN TO US OR BELIEVE WHAT WE WERE GOING THROUGH, ONLY IF THERE WAS ONE PERSON THAT WE COULD HAVE GONE TO SOMEONE THAT WOULD HAVE BEEN THERE FOR US TO

BELIEVE WHAT WE HAVE TO SAY, AND WHAT WE FEEL IN OUR HEARTS AND WITH A VERY OPEN MIND BUT MOST IMPORANTLY AN UNDERSTANDING OF OUR ABUSE AND FEAR. ANDREA THAT WOULD HAVE BEEN GREAT T HAVE SOMEONE YOU CAN TRUST TO TURN TO IN TIME OF NEED BUT WHO WOULD THAT PERSON BE THAT WE CAN TURN TO, WILL RANDY THAT PERSON WOULD BE ME, IM CONFUSED HOW WOULD THAT BE YOU? I AM GOING TO BE THE ONE TO STAND FOR THESE KIDS THAT ARE BEING ABUSED AND MISTREATED BY THERE PARENTS. NO COULD HELP US SO NOW I WILL HELP THESES KIDS I AM GOING BACK TO SCHOOLL TO FINISH AT THE TOP OF MY CLASS AND GO TO COLLEGE AND STUDY CRIMINAL JUSTICE, RANDY NEED SOMEONE TO HELP THEM ALL THE TIME BUT ALOT OF KIDS ARE SCARED TO SAY ANYTHING, CAUSE THEY THINK NO ONE WILL BELIEVE THEM OR THEY WILL NOT SAY ANYTHING BECAUSE THEY ARE TO EMBARRASS TO SAY SOMETHING. WILL I AM GOING TO HELP EVERYONE I CAN AS ANDREA TELLS RANDY THIS RANDY SPOKE SAYING IF YOIU CAN DO IT THEN I WILL GO BACK WITH YOU, AND THE BOTH OF US WILL GO TO COLLEGE AND STUDY LAW, AND GET OUR DEGREE IN CRIMINAL JUSTICE AFTER WE BOTH AGREED ON OUR FUTRE IT WAS TIME FOR RANDY TO GET READY FOR HIS MEAL, ANDREA THANK GOD MY THERAPY CAME OUR GREAT. AS RANDY WAS TALKING, I COULD NOT IMAGINE THE PAIN HE WAS GOING THREW FROM THE START OF HIS TERRIBLE ACCIDENT THAT WAS CAUSED BY A PERSON WITH NO HEART, BUT HIS DAY WILL COME WHEN RANDY GET'S OUT OF THE HOSPITAL BUT RIGHT NOW THE MOST IMPORTANT THING IS FOR RANDY TO GET BETTER, SO HE CAN GET RELEASE JUST A FEW MORE DAYS TIL THIS WEEK IS OVER WITH, AS I LOOK AT RANDY I WAS THINKING TO MYSELF WHAT WOULD HAVE BECOME OF MY LIFE IF RANDY WOULD HAVE NOT BEEN APART OF IT, I MIGHT NOT HAVE BEEN HERE RIGHT NOW HE HAS TRULY SAVED MY LIFE AS I HAVE SAVED HIM WE GIVE THANKS TO JESUS CHRIST FOR SAVING BOTH OF US. JESUS, I KNOW THAT WHATEVER HAPPENS IN OUR LIVES YOU ARE IN CONTROL FOR YOU ARE OUR LORD AND SAVIOR, AND WITHOUT YOU OUR LIVES IS NOTHING AND WITH YOU OUR LIVES IS COMPLETE AS I SIT HERE AND LOOK AT RANDY, I CLOSE MY EYES FOR A MOMENT AND JUST THINKING ABOUT THE FIRST DAY WE TALKED, WE WERE SO HAPPY AND DEEPLY IN LOVE THERE WAS NOTHING THAT MEANT MORE TO ME THAN THAT DAY. WHEN OUR HEARTS BOUDED AS ONE AND I THANK JESUS CHRIST FOR BRINGING US TOGETHER, I PRAY EVERYDAY FOR RANDY THAT ALL WILL TURN OUT WILL BUT I KNOW GOD IS IN CONTROL THERE IS SO MUCH GOING THREW MY HEAD RIGHT NOW WITH THE TRAIL COMING UP NEXT WEEK AND RANDY GOING THREW THERAPY, THIS WOULD BE MORE THAN ONE PERSON COULD HANDLE BUT I WILL BE OK AS LONG AS WE ARE TOGETHER

THERE IS NOTHING WE CAN NOT DO, I JUST NEED RANDY TO GET BETTER SO I CAN TAKE HIM HOME AND TAKE CARE OF HIM AS I AM REMINDED THERE IS ONLY 3 DAY'S LEFT BEFORE HE IS ABLE TO GO HOME, THAT IS AFTER THE DR. TELL US THAT HE IS RELEASED YES LORD LET IT BE GOOD NEWS FROM THIS DAY FORWARD.

CHAPTER 6   LOVE CONQUERS ALL

AS RANDY FINISHES HIS DINNER THE DOCTOR COMES INTO THE ROOM AND SAY'S RANDY, I AM SO PROUD OF YOU I AM HAPPY TO SAY THAT YOU WILL BE GOING HOME BY THE END OF THE WEEK.AS RANDY AND ANDREA SIT THERE WITH TIM IN THE ROOM SPEECHLESS, OF EVERYTHING THAT IS HAPPENING AND EVERYTHING THAT IS ABOUT TO HAPPEN WITH ANDREA HAVING TO GO TO COURT TO GET HER JUSTICE AND RANDY'S THERAPY FALLING INTO PLACE. THEY BOTH HAVE LOT'S OF MEMORIES OF THERE LIEVESS THAT THEY DO NOT WANT TO REMEMBER AND PARTS OF THEIR LIVES THAT THEY WISH WOULD NEVER END. RANDY'S THERAPY IS ALMOST OVER, YOU KNOW RANDY I WAS THINKING AND THE WORD LOVE IS JUST A NOUN WELL THAT IS WHAT ITS BEEN ALL MY LIFE JUST A NOUN PEOPLE WOULD TELL ME THEY LOVED ME BUT NEVER SHOWED ME, BUT WHAT WAS SHOWN IN MY LIFE WAS ACTION VERBS BY MY PARENTS WITH ALL THE HATE THEY SHOWED ME BUT YOU RANDY ONLY YOU SHOWED ME WHAT TRUE LOVE IS, YOU WERE THERE FOR ME WHEN NOBODY ELSE WAS YOU STAYED BY BEDSIDE WHEN I ALMOST DIED. AND YOU ENCOURAGED ME WHEN OTHER'S LET ME DOWN YOUR LOVE FOR ME IS MORE THAN JUST AND ACTION VERB IT IS ENTERNITY, AS I TOLD RANDY THIS, HE LOOK AT ME AND SAID AS LONG AS WE HAVE EACH OTHER WE HAVE THE WORLD. AND WITH THAT NOTHING IS IMPOSSIBEL AFTER RANDY TOLD ANDREA THAT THEY BOTH LOOKED AT TIM HE HAD TEARS IN HIS EYES THEY ASKED HIM WHAT WAS GOING ON WHY THE TEARS. I NEVER KNEW TWO POEPLE MORE IN LOVE THAN THE BOTH OF YOU MY BEST FRIENDS DEEEPLY IN LOVE THAT IS GREAT, I AM VERY HAPPY FOR YALL AFTER TIM SAID THAT RANDY GRABBED ANDREA HAND OK MY LOVE IT IS ALMOST TIME FOR ME TO GO TO MY THERAPY, I FEEL THAT AFTER TODAY I SHOULD BE GOING HOME REAL SOON AS I SAID THIS ANDREA WAS LOOKING AT ME WITH TEARS IN HER EYES. WHAT IS GOING ON ANDREA MY LOVE I ALMOST LOST YOU I CAN NOT LOSE YOU I PROMISE THAT YOU WILL

NEVER LOOSE ME, WE NEED TO GET THE COPS TO COME TO THE HSOPITAL SO YOU CAN FILE CHARGES ON JOEL FOR WHAT HE DID TO YOU, JUSTICE WILL BE SERVED FOR YOU AS IT HAS BEEEN FOR ME, I AM STILL KIND OF SCARED TO GO TO THE COURTHOUSE NEXT WEEK BUT IS SOMETHING THAT MUST BE DONE. RANDY THEY CAN NOT GO FREE AND HURT OTHER KIDS I MUST PUT A STOP TO THEM THEIR EVILNESS YES ANDREA YOU ARE RIGHT MY LOVE WE DO NEED TO GET THE COPS INVOLVED IN THIS AND JOEL CAN SHARE A CELL WITH YOUR PARENTS AFTER RANDY TOLD ME THIS I WENT TO CALL THE POLICE I TOLD THE COPS THAT I WANT TO REPORT AN ATTEMPTED MURDER ON MY FIANCE RANDY GARCIA AND SHE ASK ME WHEN DID THIS HAPPENDED? WHERE IS HE AT THIS PRESENT MOMENT I TOLD HER IT HAPPENDED WEEKS AGO, RANDY JUST CAME OUT OF A COMA A FEW DAYS AGO AND HE IS READY TO PRESS CHARGES HE KNOWS WHO HIT HIM WITH THE CAR, AFTER I TOLD THE OFFICER THIS SHE ASKED FOR DETAILS OF WHERE RANDY WAS AND WHAT HOSPITAL WE WERE AT I TOLD HER AWE ARE AT MEMORIAL HOSPITAL. IN ROOM 237, THEN SHE SAID OK I AM SENDING AN OFFICER TO GET A STATEMENT AFTER WE HUNG UP I WAS WALKING TOWARDS THE ROOM, THINKING IT FELT LIKE IT WAS HAPPENING ALL OER AGAIN AS IT DID THE FIRST TIME WITH MY PARENTS FIRST AND NOW RANDY THIS IS A CRAZY WORLD WE LIVE IN, THANKS TO OUR LORD AND SAVIROR JESUS CHRIS WE HAVE BEEN ABLE TO OVERCOME EVERYTHING THAT WE BEEN GOING THREW, AS I WALKED INTO THE ROOM I TOLD RANDY I CALLED THE POLICE. THEY ARE SENDING AN OFFICER TO GET A STATEMENT RANDY LOOKED AT ME AND DID NOT SAY A WORD, I WAS CONFUSED HE HAD A LOOK AS IF I DID SOMETHING WRONG, ARE YOU OK SAYING IN A SOFT VOICE ARE YOU UPSET WITH ME THAT I CALLED THE COPS THEN HE SAID NO MY LOVE. I AM GLAD YOIU DID AND SPEAKING ABOUT IT IS GOING TO BRING BACK MEMORIES FROM THAT DAY BUT IF YOU CAN DO IT, I KNOW I CAN TOO, AFTER RANDY SAID THAT THE NURSE CAME IN AND ASK RANDY OK MR. GARCIA ARE YOU READY TO GO FOR YOUR THERAPY? IF YOU DO GOOD TODAY, I WILL RECOMMEND THAT YOU GO HOME TOMORROW WHEN THE NURSE SAID THAT TEARS OF JOY FILLED BOTH OUR EYES, WE WENT TO THE THERAPY I SAW AS RANDY JUMPED OUT OF HIS WHEELCHAIR AND ASKED THE THERAPST OK WHAT'S FIRST I GOT THIS. SHE SMILED AND SAID OK FIRST SIT HERE AND LIFT THE 20 LBS WITH YOUR LEGS LET'S SEE HOW MANY TIMES YOU CAN LIFT THEM; OK IT IS A PIECE OF CAKE; I SAT DOWN AND LIFTED THE WEIGHTS 20 TIMES WITHOUT A PROBLEM I LOOKED UP ANDREA WAS JUST LOOKNG AT ME WITH JOY IN HER EYES. THE THERAPIST SAID VERY WELL COME AND STAND HERE SO I DID AS SHE ASKED THEN SHE SAID OK DO 20 SQUADS WITH MY ARMS EXENDED IN FRONT OF ME, I TOOK A

DEEP BREATH AND SAID OK HERE IT GOES SHE ASKED FOR 20 I GAVE HER 25. SHE LOOKED SURPRISED AND SAID WILL DONE RANDY YOU ARE DOING VERY WELL NOW ONE LAST TEST, AND THIS TEST WILL DETERMINED EVERYTHING WHCH IS THE MOST IMPORTANT TEST OF THEM ALL. I TOOK ANOTHER DEEP BREATH I LOOKED AT ANDREA SHE SHOOK HER HEAD AS IF SAYING YOU GOT THIS MY LOVE, I BELIEVE IN YOU I TOLD THE THERAPIST OF I AM READY FOR ANNYTHING SHE SAID OK GRAB THESE 15 LBS WEIGHTS AND FOLLOW ME, WE ALL WALK OUT TO THE HALL AND WENT TO THE STAIRS ON THE OTHER SIDE OF THE HALL SHE OPENED THE DOOR, AND SAID OK ANDREA YOU STAND IN FRONT OF HIM AND I WILL STAND BEHIND. NOW RANDY IF YOU NEED TO TAKE YOUR TIME PLEASE DO I NEED YOU TO WALK DOWN 2 FLIGHS OF STARIS AND BACK UP, WITH THESE WEIGHTS BY YOUR SIDE AS SHE SAID THIS I STOOD AT THE EDGE OF THE FIRST STEP WITH ANDREA IN FRON OF ME, SHE TOLD ME I GOT YOU AND THOSES WERE ALL THE WORDS I NEEDED TO HEAR. I STARTED GOING DOWN THE STAIRS AND TO MY SURPRISE THERE WAS NO PAIN I WAS ABLE TO WALK BOTH FLIGHTS OF STARIS WHEN WE WERE DONE THE NNURSE TOOK ME BACK TO MY ROOM,AND SAID OK THE DR. WILL BE IN LATER TO TALK TO YOU AND HE WILL HAVE A FULL THERAPY REPORT OF WHAT WE DID TODAY, AS I WAS GETTING INTO MY BED THE OFFICER ARRIVED HE STOOD AT THE DOOR SILENT AS HE STOOD THERE ANDREA AND RANDY TALKED ABOUT THEIR LIVES AS IT HAS BEEN UP TO THAT POINT. HOW THEY HAD SUFFER AT THE HANDS OF OTHER PEOPLE THEY WERE BOTH IN TEARS BUT NEVER GIVING UP HOPE OF WHAT IS TO COME THE POLICE LISTEN TO IT ALL AND COULD NOT HELP IT HE WAS ALSO IN TEARS, HE WAS TOUCHED BY WHAT THEY WERE SAYING HOW THEY CARED FOR EACH OTHER SO MUCH AS THE POLICE INTRODUCED HIMSLEF BOTH RANDY AND ANDREA SAID HELLO AND INVITED HIM TO SIT DOWN, HE TOLD RANDY THE STATEMENT THAT YOU WILL GIVE ME TODAY WILL PUT THIS PERSON AWAY FOR A LONG TIME I ASSURE YOU I WILL TRUST AND BELIEVE ALL YOU TELL ME. WHEN HE SAID THIS ANDREA WAS RELIEVED TO HER THAT AFTER THAT RANDY STARTED TALKING HE TOLD THE POLICEMAN EVERYTHING ABOUT HOW JOEL PLANNED TO RUN HIM OVER, AND KILL HIM HE GAVE THE POLICEMAN THE LOCATION OF THE ACCIDENT AND DESCRIBED THE TRUCK JOEL WAS DRIVING. THE PLICE ASK RANDY WHY DID HE WANT TO KILL HIM AND RANDY SAID JOEL TOLD ME IF I COULD NOT HAVE ANDREA NO ONE WOULD BE WITH HER, OH I SEE OK RANDY I AM FINISHED HERE AS THE POLICE WAS LEAVING THE ROOM RANDY AND ANDREA STAYED SILENT, AS THE COP GOT TO THE DOORWAY HE TURNED AND LOOK AT RANDY AND SAID YOU ARE BLESSED AND STRONG ENOUGH TO WITH STAND WHAT YOU ARE GOING

THREW, YOU HAVE A WONDERFUL PERSON BY YOR SIDE TO HELP YOU I WILL KEEP IN TOUGH AND LET YOU KNOW HOW THE SEARCH IS GONG, AS HE LEFT THE DOCTOR CAME IN BOTH RANDY AND ANDREA LOOKED AT HIM NERVOUS ABOUT WHAT HE WAS GOING TO SAY. AS THE DR WALK UP TO RANDY ANDREA ASKED SO TELL US IS RANDY GOING HOME THE DOCTOR SMILED AND SAID WE WILL SEE, HE ASKED RANDY TO LIFT HIS LEG THE DR PUT HIS HANDS ON THE HEELS OF RANDY FEET AND THEN SAID OK RANDY PUSH AS HARD AS YOIU CAN RANDY TOOK A DEEP BREATH AND PUSHED SO HARD HE ALMOST KNOCKED THE DOCTOR DOWN. THE DR. SAID OK GRATE IT IS OFFICIAL RANDY ASKED WHAT IS WILL RANDY YOUR TIME WITH US IS DONE TOMOOROW YOIU WILL BE GOING HOME, AS HE LEFT THE ROOM BOTH ANDREA AND RANDY HUGGED EACH OTHER TIGHT AND ANDREA LOOKED AT RANDY AND SAID YOU DID IT, WILL WE GOT OVER THIS HURDLE NOW HERE COMES MONDAY AND YOU KNOW WHAT HAPPENS ON MONDAY, YES MY LOVE YOU HAVE TO GO TO COURT BUT DON'T WORRY I WILL BE RIGHT THERE BY YOUR SIDE THE WHOLE TIME I PROMISE. LOOK RANDY I AM NOT WORRIED I AM CONTENT THAT I AM DOING THIS ALL THE PAIN, THEY HAD PUT ME THREW ALL THESES YEARS. AND I HAD NO ONE MY SIDE NOW IT IS THEIR TURN TO BE ON THE OWN WITH NO ONE ON THEIR SIDE. AFTER ANDREA SAID THIS, THEY BOTH STAYED SILENT AND JUST THOUGHT ABOUT WHAT WAS FIXING TO HAPPEN IN THE NEXT FEW DAYS. TO COME THIS WILL BE ONE TRAIL THAT WILL NEVER BE FORGOTTEN THIS WILL STAY IN ANDREA HEART AND MIND FOR A VERY LONG TIME. THE TIME HAS COME FOR RANDY TO GO HOME LET'S SEE WHERE THIS JOURNEY WILL TAKE THEM, AS RANDY AND ANDREA WERE LEAVING THE HOSPITAL THE DETECTIVE SHOWED UP TO THE HOSPITAL, HE MET RANDY AND ANDEREA AT THE FRONT DOOR WILL RANDY I SEE YOU ARE FINALLY GOING HOME YES I AM AND WHY ARE YOU HERE? WILL I GOT GOOD NEWS FOR YOU. THE POLICE ARRESTED JOEL LAST NIGHT AND WE CHARGED HIM WITH ATTEMPTED MURDERE NOW RANDY WHEN IT IS TIME FOR HIM TO GO TO COURT WE NEED YOU THERE, TO TESTIFY ON WHAT HAPPENED I WILL BE THERE AS ANDREA WAS JUST LOOKING WITH A BLANK LOOK ON HER FACE, AND THEN SHE SAID WOW I CAN NOT BELIEVE ALL OF THIS IS HAPPENING SO QUICKLY THEN SHE PAUSED AND SAID WILL FIRST I FIND OUT THE TRUTH ABOUT MY PARENTS. AFTER ALL THAT HAS HAPPENED AS I GET BACK TO TOWN I FOUND MY BOYFRIEND HERE AT THE HOSPITAL CAUSE THIS BOY TRIED TO BE WITH ME, AND I TURNED HIM AWAY SO I COULD BE WITH THE ONE PERSON THAT I LOVE NOW I HAVE TO GO TO COURT NEXT WEEK, AND RANDY IS GING TO GO TO COUR REAL SOON AS WILL I WONDER WHEN IS ALL OF THIS GOING TO END? WHEN ARE WE GOING TO FINALLY BE HAPPY WHEN LORD. I TURNED AND

SAID TO ANDRAE LET US GO HOME I GRABBED HER HAND AND WE LEFT THE HOSPITAL, THE REST OF THE WEEKEND WE STAYED SILENT WE DID NOT TALK ALL WE COULD DO WAS THINK ABOUT WHAT WILL HAPPEN NEXT WEEK, WILL HER PARENTS GO TO PRISON OR WILL THEY BE SET FREE. WHAT WILL HAPPEN IN MY CASE WILL JOEY GO TO PRISON OR WHAT WILL HAPPEN ONLY TIME WILL TELL. AS I SIT THERE ANDREA CAME INTO THE ROOM AND I STARTED THNKING ABOUT WHAT HAPPEN AT HER HOUSE THE TORTURE AND SUFFERING HER PARENTS PUT HER THREW. I REMEMBER THE DAY SHE ALMOST DIED I FELT AS IF I WAS LOOSEN MY WHOLE WORLD, I COULD NOT IMAGINE MY LIFE WITHOUT ANDREA, I HOLD HER TIGHT THAT NIGHT AND PRAYED THAT SHE WOULD MAKE IT, I THANK GOD TH AT SHE MADE IT TH REW ALL SHE WAS GOING THREW SO NOW IS THE TIME TO ASK HER THE QUESTION I BEEN HOLDING BACK FOR SO MANY YEARS, FOR IT NEVER WAS THE RIGHT TIME TO BRING UP THE PASS, BUT I FEEL NOW I MUST KNOW THE TRUTH ANDREA MY LOVE THERE IS A QUESTION I BEEN WANTING TO ASK YOU FOR THE PASS YEARS BUT NEVER DID SO NOW I AM GOING TO ASK YOU WHAT I SHOULD OF ASK YOU 15 YEARS AGO. OK YOU KNOW YOU CAN ASK ME ANYTHING WHAT IS IT AS ANDREA SAT NEXT TO ME I LOOKED HER IN THE EYES AND SAID IT IS ABOUT THAT DAY THAT YOU WENT TO THE HOSPITAL, SHE LOOKED PUZZLED AND SAID OK WHAT ABOUT THAT DAY WILL WHEN I GOT TO YOUR HOUSE THAT DAY YOU WAS INSIDE, AND WHEN I ASKED FOR YOU ONE OF THE BOYS ASKED WHO IS ASKING AND I SAID RANDY THEN HE REPLIED OH YES ANDREA TOLD US ABOUT YOU. AND THEN I ASK HIM WHAT DO YOU MEAN SHE TOLD YOU ABOUT ME WHO ARE YOU WILL RANDY WE ARE ALL WITH HER, SHE IS WITH ANOTHER GIRL SHE GOES BOTH WAYS WE ALL HAD HER AND YOU WILL GET YOUR TURN AFTER YOU GIVE HER ENOUGH DRUGS, SO I AM ASKING YOU WHAT WAS HE TALKING ABOUT AND IS IT TRUE. SHE LOOKED AT ME WITH TEARS IN HER EYES LOOK RANDY I HAVE BEEN SUFFERING ALL MY LIFE I KEPT THE PAIN INSIDE OF ME AND LOT'S OF SECRETS I HAVE EXPERIENCE, NOW THEY WERE JUST FRIENDS NOTHING MORE, WE DID DRUGS TOGETHER I WAS NEVER INVOLVED WITH THEM YES WE HUNG OUT TOGETHER I ASSURE YOU I WAS NEVER WITH ANY OF THEM, HE WAS PLAYING WITH YOUR EMOTIONS YOUR THE ONLY ONE FOR ME I PROMISE AFTER ANDREA TOLD ME THIS I WAS RELIEVED WE CONTINUED THE REST OF THE NIGHT NERVOUSE FOR NO REASON. BUT WE KNEW WE HAD A LONG WEEEK AHEAD OF US I HOPE ANDREA IS PREPARED FOR WHAT SHE IS GOING TO FACE, I HAD TO BE PREPARED ALSO WHAT I WAS GOING TO FACE SOON BUT I KNOW THAT IT DOES NOT MATTER WHAT WE WENT THREW IN THE PASS, AND THE FUTURE IS SO CLOSE FOR WE HAVE EACH OTHER AND AS LONG AS WE HAVE EACH OTHER EVERYTHING ELSE

DOES NOT MATTER AFTER RANDY SAID THIS THEY BOTH JUST SAT THERE AND TRYED TO EAT THERE DINNER. BUT THEY WERE BOTH SO FULL OF EMOTION THEY COULD NOT EAT THEY WOULD JUST SIT THERE AND STARED INTO THE NIGHT, WITH TEARS IN THEIR EYES THEY SPOKE NOT ONE WORD THEY FINALLY WENT TO BED WITH A MIXTURE OF TEARS FIRST HAPPY TEARS THEN SAD TEARS, SOON MORNING WILL BE HERE ANDREA WILL HAVE TO GET READY TO GO TO THE ATTORNEY'S IN THE MORNING. IT'S SUNDAY HE MADE A SPECIAL TRIP TO HIS OFFICE TO MAKE SURE ANDREA IS READY AND PREPARED FOR WHAT IS GOING TO HAPPEN, MONDAY MORINING THERE ARE LOT'S OF THINGS THEY MUST GO THREW TO BE READY FOR WHAT ANDREA IS ABOUT TO FACE. AS SHE WALKS INTO THE ATTORNEY'S OFFICE, HE SAID HELLO I AM ATTORNEY REYES I WILL BE YOUR ATTORNEY THREW OUT THIS TRAIL AGAINST YOUR PARENTS. I HAVE TO ASK YOIU SOME QUESTIONS OK MR. REYES ASK FIRST ARE YOU TELLING THE TRUTH ABOUT EVERYTHING YOU STATED WHAT YOUR PARENTS DID TO YOU, AS THE ATTORNEY SAID THIS ANDREA HAD A LOOKED ON HER FACE AND AS SHE STANDS UP TO WALK OUT THE ATTORNEY STOP HER WAIT ANDREA DON'T LEAVE, WHY NOT YOU DON'T BELIEVE ME IF I DID NOT BELIEVE YOU I WOULD HAVE NOT TAKEN YOUR CASE. AS ANDREA SITS BACK DOWN THE ATTORNEY ASK AGAIN SO ANDREA ARE YOU TELLING THE TRUTH ON WHAT YOU SAID YOUR PARENTS DID TO YOU ANDREA STAY SILENT AS THE ATTORNEY READS THE POLICE STATEMENT, HIS HEAD JUST DROPPED HE COULD NOT BELIEVE WHAT HE WAS READING HE COULD NOT SAY A WORD THEN HE LOOKED OUT THE WINDOW, AND JUST STOOD THERE WITH A LOOK ON HIS FACE OF SADNESS AND THEN HE LOOK AT ANDREA AND HE WAS SILENT THEN ANDREA ASK HIM ARE YOU OK, CAN YOU HELP ME TO GET JUSTICE YES ANDREA I CAN HELP YOU IT IS JUST THAT I NEVER HEARD OF A PARENT COULD TREAT THEIR CHILDREAN LIKE THIS. I ASSURE YOU ANDREA YOU WILL GET JUSTICE AND I WILL GIVE YOUR PARENTS THE MAXIMA TIME IN PRISON THAT THE LAW ALLOWS, NOW YOU HAVE TO JUST BE STRONG AND TELL THE TRUTH ANDREA I AM LETTING YOU KNOW THAT THE WHOLE TIME DURING THIS TRIAL IT IS GOING TO BE ROUGH, IN THAT COURTROOM THE ATTORNEY IS GOING TO TRY AND PROVE THAT IT WAS YOUR FAULT THAT THEY NEVER HURT YOU. THAT THEY SHOWED YOU NOTHING BUT LOVE AND YOU'RE DOING THIS BECAUSE THEY DISCIPLINE YOU TO DO THE RIGHT THING, NOW WE ALL KNOW THEY WILL TRY TO CONVINCE THE JURY THAT THEY ARE INNOCENT BUT I WILL PROVE THIER GUILTY. I HAVE THE PROOF THAT THEY HURT YOU AFTER THE ATTORNEY TOLD ANDREA THAT HE PUT HIS HAND ON ANDREA SHOLDER LOOKED HER IN THE EYE, ANDREA WE ARE BY YOUR SIDE AND WE WILL NOT LET YOU DOWN NOW

GO HOME AND GET YOUR REST I WILL SEE YOU EARLY IN THE MORING AS THEY LEFT THE ATTORNEY'S OFFICE, ANDRA STOPPED AND SAID OH NO I FORGOT HOW CAN I FORGET SHE IS GOING TO BE UPSET WITH ME ANDREA WHAT DID YOUI FORGET? WHO ARE YOU TALKING ABOUT, SARA SHE CALLED ME WHEN I WAS AT THE BUS STATION SHE TOLD ME SHE NEED TO TELL ME SOMETHING VERY IMPORTANT AND WITH EVERYTHING THAT HAS BEEN GOING ON I FORGOT TO GO TALK TO HER, WE NEED TO GO TO HER HOUSE RIGHT NOW AND SEE WHAT SHE NEEDED TO TELL ME AS THEY WERE GING TO SARA HOUSE ANDREA COULD JUST THINK AND WONDER WHAT SARA HAS TO SAY SHE WAS HOPING IT WAS NOT MORE BAD NEWS. AS THEY GOT TO HER HOUSE ANDREA COULD NOT MOVE THEN FINALLY SHE WALKED UP TO SARA DOOR BEFORE SHE HAD A CHANCE TO KNOCK SARA OPENED THE DOOR, FINALLY YOU CAME TO SEE ME YES SARA SORRY THEIR WAS SO MUCH GOING ON NOW WHAT IS IT YOU NEED TO TELL ME I KNOW YOU ARE GOING TO COURT TOMORROW, AND I WANT TO TESTIFY ON YOUR BEHALF HOW DO YOU KNOW I AM GOING TO COURT TOMORROW. AND HOW DO YOU KNOW WHAT HAPPEN TO ME YOUR OLD FRIEND OPEN UP TO ME ON EVERYTIHNG AND HE GAVE ME THE LETTERS YOU WROTE HIM, EXPLAINING IN DETAIL WHAT YOUR PARENTS DID TO YOU AND WHAT HAPPENED TO YOU HE ALSO TOOK THE LETTERS TO THE ATTORNEY. SO THAT IS WHY THE ATTORNEY TOLD ME HE HAD ALL THE PROOF HE NEEDED TO PUT THEM AWAY FOR A LONG TIME, THANK YOU AND WHO ALL READ THE LETTERS NO ONE I KEPT THEM PUT AWAY THANK YOU FOR SAVING THEM FOR ME YOU TRUELY ARE A TRUE FRIEND, I WAS IN SO MUCH PAIN WHEN I WROTE THESE LETTERS FELT LIKE MY BODY WAS TURNED INSIDE OUT.

CHAPTER 7 JUSTICE FOR ALL

I AM SO SORRY ANDREA THAT YOU HAD TO EXPERIANCE THAT IN THE HANDS OF YOUR PARENTS THANK YOU SARA I HAVE A QUESTION DID YOU EVER PLAN ON GIVING ME THESE LETTERS, YES I WAS JUST HOLDING ONTO THEM FOR YOU I FELT IF I HAD GIVEN THEM TO YOU AT THE WRONG TIME YOU MIGHT HAVE DESTROYED THEM, TO GET THE MEMORIES OUT OF YOUR HEAD OF THOSE TERRIBLE TIMES IN YOUR LIFE YES YOU ARE RIGHT I TRYED SO MANY TIMES TO GET THOSE DAY'S OUT OF MY HEAD. BUT IT IS NOT THAT EASY TO FORGET ALL THE ABUSE I SUFFER FOR SO MANY YEARS AND IF YOU WOULD HAVE GIVEN ME THE LETTERS, I WOULD HAVE TORN THEM UP AND BURNED THEM IT WAS A GREAT IDEAL THAT YOU KEPT THEM FROM ME, THESE LETTERS ARE GOING TO HELP IN THE PROCESS OF SENDING MY PARENTS AWAY FOR A VERY LONG TIME, SO TELL ME WHEN YOU READ THEM WHAT DID YOU THINK AND WHAT DID YOU FEEL WHAT WAS THE FIRST THOUGHT THAT CAME TO MIND, I SHOULD GO TO THE COPS THEN I DECIDED I WANTED TO JUST GET SOME FRIENDS AND GO TO YOUR HOUSE AND KILL YOUR PARENTS FOR DOING THAT TO YOU AND HURTING YOU. THEY DO KNOW THAT YOU ARE A GIFT FROM GOD YOU ARE A GREAT PERSON THAT DESERVES LOVE AND HAPPINESS NOT PAIN AND SUFFERING AS THEY DID TO YOU, BUT THEY WILL PAY FOR WHAT THEY DID TO YOU SARA YOU ARE TRULY A GREAT FRIEND I GOTTA GO BUT I WILL SEE YOU IN THE MORNING, AT THE COURTHOUSE OK ANDREA HAVE A GOOD NIGHT SEE YOU TOMORROW ON THEIR WAY HOME ANDREA TOLD RANDY WILL IT LOOKS

LIKE THINGS ARE GOING TO FINALLY GO MY WAY AND I WILL GET MY LIFE BACK, ANDREA YOU ARE BLESSED TO HAVE SO MANY PEOPLE THAT CARE ABOUT YOU AND LOVE YOU AS WE ALL DO. THANK YOU RANDY FOR GIVING ME YOUR LIFE AND BEING A PART OF MY LIFE AS WE GET TO OUR HOUSE WE DID NOT EVEN EAT DINNER WE JUST GOT READY TO GO TO BED WE HAD TO BE AT THE COURT EARLY IN THE MORNING AND WE DID NOT WANT TO BE LATE, AS RANDY LOOKS AT ANDREA HE TELLS HER GOODNIGHT AS THEY SAID THERE GOODNIGHTS THERE WAS A SMILE ON ANDREA FACE THAT NO ONE HAS SEEN IN A LONG TIME, SHE HAD THAT GLADNESS IN HER HEART THAT SHE BEEN WAITING FOR SO MANY YEARS AND NOW AFTER SO MUCH SUFFERING IN HER LIFE SHE WILL FINALLY BE SET FREE FROM IT ALL. MORNING HAS ARRIVED LET'S SEE HOW THIS DAY GOES AS THEY WAKE UP RANDY SPEAKS FIRST GOOD MORNING ANDREA; HOW DID YOU SLEEP; WILL I COULD NOT REALLY SLEEP I JUST KEPT THINKING ABOUT EVERYTHING BUT LET'S GET READY TO GO WE WILL PICK UP SOMETHING TO EAT ON THE WAY TO THE COURT HOUSE. I AM MY LOVE AND THIS IS YOUR SPECIAL DAY. YOU HAVE BEEN WAITING FOR ALL OF YOUR LIFE THE DAY WHEN YOU'RE HEALING AND HAPPINESS START RANDY TO TELL YOU THE TRUTH THE DAY THAT MY HAPPINESS STARTED WAS A LONG TIME AGO THAT IS THE DAY YOU CAME INTO MY LIFE, YOU HAVE ALWAYS BEEN THERE WITH ME AND BY MY SIDE NO MATTER WHAT HAPPENS IN COURT I ALREADY WON THE BATTLE CAUSE IT DOESN'T MATTER WHAT THEY DID TO ME OR HOW HEY ABUSED ME. THEY NEVER COULD BREAK ME YES I WAS HEARTBROKEN BUT NOT BROKEN UP TO THE POINT OF NO RETURN YES ANDREA YOU STARYED STRONG THREW THIS WHOLE ORDEAL, I LOVE YOU AND I AM VERY PROUD OF YOU FOR THE STEPS YOU ARE TAKING FOR JUSTICE WE JUST MADE IT TO THE COURTHOUSE ARE YOU READY TO GO IN LOOKING AT RANDY WITH A BIG SMILE ON HER FACE, I AM READY TO GO FACE THESE MONSTERS LET'S GO DO T HIS THEY BOTH WALK INTO THE BUILDING AS ANDREA WAS WALKING TOWARDS THE COURTROOM SHE SAW THE COPS TAKING HER PARENS INTO THE COURTROOM. IN THERE ORANGE JAIL CLOTHES AND HANDCUFFS SHE JUST SMILED AND SAID NOW YOU SEE HOW IT FEELS TO BE IN THE LOCKDOWN, WITH NO ONE TO HELP YOU ANDREA MOM SPOKE TO HER HOW COULD YOU DO THIS TO YOUR MOM AND DAD WE LOVE YOU WHY ARE YOU DOING THIS, SERIOUSLY YOU GOING TO SIT THERE WITH A STRAIGHT FACE AND SAY YOU LOVE ME HOW DARE YOU SAY THAT TO ME, ANDREA ME AND YOUR DAD DO LOVE YOU SHUT UP MOM THE ONLY THING THE BOTH OF YOU LOVED WAS DOING YOUR DRUGS AND ABUSED ME EVERY DAY OF MY LIFE, THEN ALLOW OTHER MEN TO BE ALL OVER ME HOW DARE YOU SAY YOU ARE MY MOM AND CARE ABOUT ME IM IN TEARS AND HURT,

HOW COULD YOU ALLOW OTHER MAN TO COME TO MY ROOM I WAS ONLY 11 YEARS OLD, THEN THE WORST PART YOU ALLOWED YOUR HUSBAND TO HAVE HIS WAY WITH ME YOU BOTH ARE VERY SICK. AND YOU BOTH WILL GET WHAT YOU HAVE COMING TO THE BOTH OF YALL COME ON RANDY LET'S GO, WILL MR AND MRS. GARCIA I HAVE YOU KNOW THAT ANDREA HATES THE BOTH OF YOU WITH A PASSION, AND WHO ARE YOU I AM ATTORNEY REYES AND I PROMISE YOU I WILL DO MY BEST TO PUT THE BOTH OF YOU UNDER THE JAIL AND THROUGH AWAY THE KEY, AS RANDY AND ANDREA TAKE THEIR SEATS THERE IS A SILENCE IN THE COURTROOM THEN THE POLICE SPEAKS ALL RISE THE DISTRICT COURT IS NOW IN SESSION, THE HONORABLE JUDGE WRIGHT PRESIDING YOU MAY BE SEATED AS WE SIT DOWN THE JUDGE LOOKS AT ANDREA CASE SHAKES HIS HEAD, AS HE LOOKS AT ANDREA PARENTS WITH A DISBELIFE AND A MEAN LOOK AS THE JUDGE SPEAKS SAYING MR AND MRS GARCIA YOU BOTH ARE CHARGE WITH ENDANGERMENT TO A CHILD, ALONG WITH ABUSED AND INAPPROPRIATE BEHAVIOR CAUSEING ANDREA GARCIA THE LOST OF HER INNOCENCE IN THE HANDS OF HER DAD. HOW DO YOU BOTH PLEAD THERE ATTORNEY SAYS NOT GUILTY WHEN HE SAID THAT HE SAW THE LOOK ON ANDREA FACE SHE WANTED TO SPEAK, I TOLD HER NO DON'T JUST WAIT YOU WILL SEE EVERYTHING WILL BE OK I PROMISE YOU THAT YOU WILL GET YOUR CHANCE TO SPEAK, THE BAIL WILL BE SET AT THE JUDGE STAYED SILENT FOR A BIT LOOKING AT THE FILE THEN SAID THERE WILL BE NO BAIL THIS MATTER WILL BE GOING TO TRAIL BY JURY TAKE THEM AWAY. THE BAILIFF CAME UP AND TOOK THEM BOTH AWAY AS THEY WERE LEAVING YOU COULD SEE THE RELIFE ON ANDREA FACE, AS HER PARENTS WERE GOING BACK TO THEIR CELL THE ATTORNEY WENT UP TO THE JUDGE AND INFORMED HIM THAT THERE WAS ANOTHER YOUNG GIRL, THAT THEY HAD KIDNAPPED AS HE WAS TELLING THE JUDGE AS THE ATTORNEY WAS EXPLAINING THIS MATTER, THE JUDGE STOPPED HIM AND ASK HOW WAS THE GIRL THE ATTORNEY LOOKED INTO THE FILES AND SAID SHE WAS ONLY 12 YEARS OLD YOUR HONOR. AS HE LOOKED AT THE JUDGE, HE HAD AN ANGER ON HIS FACE THAT NO ONE HAS EVER SEEN YOUR HONOR WITH YOUR PREMISSION WE WOULD LIKE TO ADD THIS TO OUR EVIDENCE. YES, HAVE ALL YOUR DOCUMENTS IN ORDER WE DO NOT WANT A MISTRIAL AND THEY ARE SET FREE NO YOUR HONOR I WILL MAKE SURE THEY WILL BE IN ORDER, AND THE PEOPLE WILL BE READY WE ALSO HAVE WITNESSES AND LETTERS TO PROVE MY CLIENTS STATEMENT. GOOD WE NEED ALL THE EVIDENCE YOU HAVE ON THESE TWO CASES THAT IS ALL COURT WILL RESUME 9 AM YES, YOUR HONOR. AS THE ATTORNEY LEFT THE COURTHOUSE HE WENT STRAIGHT TO ANDERA HOUSE AS ANDREA OPEN THE DOOR THE ATTORNEY

TOLD HER I HAVE GOOD NEWS, THE JUDGE IS ALLOWING TO PRESENT THE CASE OF WHEN YOUR PARENTS KIDNAPPED THAT OTHER GIRL THAT IS GREAT, YES I HAVE TO GO TO HER HOUSE TO TRY AND GET HER TO TESTIFY I WILL GO WITH YOU AND TALK TO HER ALSO THESE TWO MONSTERS TOOK ADVANTAGE OF A LOT OF PEOPLE AND HURT LOTS OF PEOPLE, OK ANDREA YOU AND RANDY CAN GO WITH ME TO HER HOUSE THIS WILL BE A BIG HELP, WE NEED ALL THE HELP WE CAN GET YOU GO INSIDE WITH ME TO TALK TO HER AND HER PARENTS, OK I WILL DO ANYTHING NEEDED TO BE DONE TO GET HER TO GO AND TESTIFY THE ATTORNEY KNOCKS ON THE DOOR HER PARENS ANSER HELLO HOW CAN I HELP YOU. HELLO, MY NAME IS WAIT WE KNOW WHO YOU ARE WE KNOW YOU ALSO ANDREA COME IN PLEASE NOW WHAT CAN WE DO FOR YOU, WE NEED YOUR DAUGHTER JUDY TO TESTIFY AT THE TRAIL I DONT THINK THAT WILL BE A GOOD IDEAL SHE IS STILL TRAUMATIZED FROM WHAT HAPPENENED, SHE IS NOT HERSELF NO MORE. SHE STILL WAKES UP AT NIGHT CRYING AND SCARED OF THE THINGS THAT WEERE DONE TO HER, HOW LONG WAS SHE GONE HOW LONG DID THEY HAVE HER SHE WENT THREW TORTURE FOR 6 MONTHS. ANDREA LOOKS DOWN THEN LOOKS AT HER PARENTS TRY 4 YEARS OF TORTURE AND ABUSE AND ANYTHING YOU CAN IMAGINE, IT STARTED WHEN I WAS A VERY YOUNG GIRL I HAD JUST TURNED 9 YEARS OLD ALL THE WAY TIL I WAS 12 YEARS OLD CAN I PLEASE GO TALK TO HER, WHERE IS JUDY SHE IS IN HER ROOM AND WE ARE DEEPLY SORRY FOR ALL THE PAIN AND SUFFERING THAT YOU WENT THREW THANKS YOIU EXCUSE ME. I AM GOING TO TALK TO JUDY AS ANDREA KNOCKS ON JUDY DOOR SHE HEARS HER STRATING TO CRY AND SAYING NO PLEASE LEAVE ME ALONE DONT HURT ME NO MORE, JUDY IT IS ME ANDREA LET ME COME IN AND TALK TO YOU SHE WAS SILENT FOR A BIT THEN SHE FINALLY OPEN THE DOOR MAY I COME IN AND SIT WITH YOU FOR A WHILE, AND TALK TO YOU YES ANDREA COME IN AND WHAT ARE YOU DOING HERE AT MY HOUSE WE BOTH HAVE THE SAME PROBLEM. HOW HAVE YOU BEEN DOING WILL ANDREA HONESTLY I DONT KNOW ANYMORE I AM STILL IN SHOCK FROM WHAT HAPPEN AND EVERYNIGHT I HAVE DREAMS, OF WHAT THEY DID TO ME I KNOW WHAT YOU MEAN I STILL HAVE DREAMS OF THOSE DAYS AS ANDREA SITS IN JUDY ROOM SHE LOOKS AROUND THEN TELLS JUDY WOW YOU HAVE A NICE ROOM, IT SAYS YOU HAVE LOTS OF LOVE IN THIS HOUSE YOU KNOW IN MY OLD ROOM THERE WAS NOTHING BUT PAIN AND SUFFERING, MY DAD AND ALL OF HIS FRIENDS WOULD HAVE THEIR WAY WITH ME AND MY MOM WOULD JUST LAUGH AT ME, I NEVER KNOW WHAT A FATHER AND MOTHER LOVE WAS I WAS NEVER ABLE TO EXPERIENCE THAT LIFE OF HAPPINESS. THE KIIND OF STUFFED I EXPERIENCESD SHOLD NOT HAPPENDED TO A LITTLE GIRL I WAS JUST 12 YEARS

OLD JUDY I KNOW EXACTLY HOW YOU FEEL, NOW FROM WHAT THEY DID TO YOU AND IT IS NOT YOUR FAULT THIS HAPPENED TO YOU IT IS ALL THEIR FAULT WHCIH IS WHY I NEED YOU TO OME TO COURT WITH ME, AND HELP PUT THEM AWAY SO WILL YOU JOIN ME IN THIS FIGHT FOR JUSTICE, AS ANDREA ASKED JUDY THIS SHE STAYED SILENT GOT UP AND WALKED TOWARDS THE WINDOW LOOKING OUT INTO SPACE. THEN AS SHE TURNS TO ANDREA, SHE SAID WITH TEARS IN HER EYES I WOULD LOVE TO GO TO COURT WITH YOU AND PUT THEM AWAY BUT I DONT WANT TO SEE THEM NO MORE I AM SCARED, I KNOW YOU ARE SCARED I BEEN SCARED FOR MANY YEARS BUT THE BEST WAY TO FIGHT YOUR FEAR IS MOVE FORWARD WITH WHAT MUST BE DONE TO GET JUSTICE, YOUR RIGHT ANDREA OK LETS DO THIS AND PUT THESE MONSTERS AWAY GREAT I WILL LET YOUR PARENTS KNOW YOU WILL BE COMING TO COURT WITH US IN THE MORNING. THANK YOU, FOR TAKING YOUR STAND IN THIS FIGHT AGAINST THESE EVIL PEOPLE WE WILL SEE YOU IN THE MORNING AS THEY LEFT JUDY HOUSE, THEY JUST LOOOKED AT EACH OTHER WITH A SMILE OF VICTORY THE REST OF THE NIGHT WAS THEIR BEST NIGHT EVER. SINCE ALL THIS HAD BEGAN THIS WAS THE FIRST NIGHT THAT ANDREA WAS ABLE TO SLEEP IN PEACE AS THE ATTORNEY SAID HIS GOOD NIGHTS TO ANDREA AND RANDY HE WAS JUST SMILING AS HE SAID TO ANDREA YOU DID IT, I WILL SEE THE BOTH OF YOU IN THE MORNING GOODNIGHT MR REYES AS THEY CONTINUE TO WALK TO THEIR HOUSE THEY DID NOT SAY A WORD, BUT THE LOOK IN THERE EYES SAID IT ALL THEY WERE FULL OF JOY AND HAPPINESS IN THEIR HEARTS ANDREA NEW THE FIGHT JUST STARTED, BUT SHE ALREADY SAW VICTORY AS SOON AS THEY GOT TO THEIR HOUSE THEY WENT RIGHT TO BED AS THEY SLEPT THE NIGHT WENT BY SO QUICKLY, AS THEY GOT UP IN THE MORNING THEY RUSH TO GET TO THE COURTHOUSE TO MEET EVERYONE BEFORE THE TRIAL STARTED, AS RANDY SPEAKS TO ANDREA IT IS ALMOST TIME TO GO ARE YOU READY. YES I AM READY TO GO LET'S GO I CANNOT WAIT TO GET THERE AND GET THIS OVER WITH I HOPE JUDY ARRIVES ON TIME OK MY LOVE I WILL GET THE STUFF READY AND I WILL MEET YOIU OUTSIDE. OK HERE I COME AS THEY LEFT THE HOUSE AND HEADED TOWARDS THE COURTHOUSE, THEY SAW TIM COMING DOWN THE ROAD, HE STOPPED AND ASKED THEM ARE YOU ALL HEADING TO THE COURTHOUSE WE ARE ON OUR WAY THERE RIGHT NOW. COME ON LET'S GO I WILL TAKE YALL THERE WHY ARE YOU HERE WHAT HAPPENED NOTHING I JUST KNOW I NEEDED TO BE HERE, WE WERE PLEASED THAT TIM CAME BACK AS WE GOT TO THE COURTHOUSE, WE SAW JUDY AND HER PARENTS. WERE OUTSIDE TALKING TO THE ATTORNEY WE PARKED AND RUSHED TO WHERE THEY WERE ANDREA YOU MADE IT ON TIME, SO THIS IS HOW IT IS GOING TO GO FOR YOUR

PARENTS I WILL BE CALLING THEM TO THE STAND FIRST AND AFTER I QUESTION THEM, I WILL CALL YOU TO THE STAND AND WHEN YOU TESTIFY I WILL MENTION THE LETTERS ONE AT A TIME, AND YOU WILL EXPLAIN TO THE COURT EXACTLY WHAT HAPPENED IN THE LETTTER I KNOW IT IS GOING TO BE HARD ON YOU BUT YOU HAVE TO DO IT, OK I WILL I AM READY FOR THIS AS I SAID BEFORE I WOULD DO ANYTHING AND EVERYTHING I HAVE TO DO TO GET JUSTICE FOR WHAT THEY DID TO ME. OK GOOD AND AS FOR JUDY I MIGHT CALL YOU TO THE STAND TODAY OR TOMORROW JUST BE READY WHEN I DO, AND DOES RANDY KNOW EVERYTHING THAT HAPPENDED TO YOU NO NOT EVERYTHNG JUST WHAT I TOLD HIM AND HE WAS THERE FOR ME WHEN I ALMOST DIED, AND HE OVER HEARD MY PARENTS WHEN THEY SAID THEY WISHED I HAD DIED RANDY WILL YOU TAKE THE STAND AND TESTIFY WHAT YOU SAW AND HEARD? YES, I WILL TELL EVERYTHING I KNOW GREAT WILL LET US GO INSIDE AS WE WALKED INTO THE COURTROOM, I SEE MY PARENTS SITTING THERE WITH A SMILE ON THEIR FACES. I WAS CONFUSED AS TO WHY THEY WERE SMILING THEY SAT THERE IN THE SAME PLACE AS WE DID, THE DAY BEFORE HERE COMES THE JUDGE ALL RISE COURT IN SESSION THE HONORABLE JUDGE WRIGHT PRESIDING ALL MAY BE SEATED, MR REYES IS YOUR CLIENT READY YES SHE IS YOUR HONOR MR. SANCHEZ ARE YOUR CLIENTS READY YES YOUR HONOR THEY ARE. MR. REYES, MAY WE HEAR YOUR OPENING STATEMENT YES, YOUR HONOR LADIES AND GENTLEMEN OF THE JURY THIS IS NOT GOING TO BE AN EASY CASE TO HEAR THERE WILL BE DISTURBING EVIDENCE BROUGHT TO LIGHT, OF HOW MY CLIENTS PARENTS PURPOSELY CAUSED BODY HARM AND MADE HER SUFFER STARTING AT THE AGE OF 9 YEARS OLD UNTIL SHE WAS 14 YEARS OLD, THE ATTORNEY STAYED SILENT THE JUDGE ASKED THE ATTORNEY TO CONTINUE HE LOOKED UP AND SAID THE WORST PART OF THIS ABUSED WAS HER DAD AND HIS FRIENDS ABUSED HER. SHE WAS SOLD TO THESE MEN FOR DRUG MONEY AS HE SAID THIS HE LOOKED AT HER PARENTS AND SAID LOOK AT THEM THEY ARE SUPPOSED TO LOVE HER, AND SHE WAS SUPPOSED TO FEEL SAFE AND PROTECTIVE IN HER OWN HOME HER DAD WAS SUPPOSED TO PROTECT HER FROM MEN INSTEAD HE INVITE THEM INTO HIS HOUSE TO HEAVE HER AS THEY PLEASE, AND THE OTHER PART HER MOM ALLOWED THIS TO HAPPEN BUT INSTEAD OF STOPPING THEM SHE JUST LAUGHED AT HER. AND SAID GET WHAT YOU DESERVE I ASKED FOR THE JURY TO RETURN THE VERDICT FOR HER DAD OF CHILD ENDANGERMENT. AND FOR HER MOM RETURNED THE VERDICT OF ACCESSORY TO CHILD ENDAGERMENT FOR ALLOWING THE ABUSE AND TORTURE OF THEIR DAUGHTER, THAT IS ALL THANK YOU AS THE ATTORNEY FINSH HE WIPES THE TEARS FROM HIS EYES I LOOKED OVER TO THE JUDGE HE

HAD TEARS IN HIS EYES. AS THE ATTORNEY SAT DOWN THE JUDGE SAID MR SANCHEZ DO YOU WISH TO PRESENT YOUR OPENING STATEMENT YES, YOUR HONOR, AS HE WALKS TOWARDS THE JURY HE SPEAKS WOW THAT IS A WILD OPENING STATEMENT PUTTING THE BLAME HER PARENTS WHEN ALL THEY DID WAS LOVE AND TRIED TO RAISED HER THE RIGHT WAY. SHE WAS OUT OF CONTROL SNEAKING OFF WITH BOYS AT ALL TIMES OF THE NIGHT, SHE GOT COUGHT SO SHE MADE UP THIS STORY SO SHE WOULD NOT GET IN TROUBLE WITH HER PARENTS. LADIES AND GENTLLMENT OF THE JURY I ASK THAT YOU BRING BACK THE VERDICT OF NOT GUILTY FOR THE MOM AND DAD WHO ARE TWO GREAT PARENTS, AS THE ATTORNEY RETURNS TO HIS SEAT NEXT TO HER PARENTS THE JUDGE TURNS TO ANDREA ATORNEY AND SAYS MR. REYES ARE YOU READY TO PROVE YOUR CASE, YES YOUR HONOR OK CALL YOUR FIRST WITNESS AS THE ATTORNEY LOOKS AT RANDY SAYS I CALL RANDY GARCIA TO THE STAND, AS RANDY GET'S UP TO GO TO THE STAND HE HAD A SURPRISED LOOK ON HIS FACE TO BE CALLED SO EARLY IN THE TRIAL AS HE GOT TO THE STAND, THE BALIFF CAME TO RANDY WITH A BIBLE IN HIS HAND PUT YOUR RIGHT HAND ON THE BIBLE AND RAISE YOIUR HAND DO YOU SWEAR TO TELL TEH TRUTH THE WHOLE TRUTH AND NOTHING BUT THE TRUTH SO HELP YOU GOD, I DO YOU MAY BE SEATED CAN YOU STATE YOUR NAME FOR THE COURT, MY NAME IS RANDY GARCIA AND HOW DO YOU KNOW ANDREA GARCIA SHE IS MY GIRLFRIEND HOW LONG HAVE YOU KNOWN HER I HAVE KNOWN ANDREA EVER SINCE TH 6TH GRADE, SHE BECAME MY GIRLFRIEND WOULD YOU SAY THAT ANDREA HAS BEEN HONEST WOULD ALWAYS TELL THE TRUTH, AS FAR AS I KNOW SHE HAS NEVER LIE TO ME OR ANYONE ELSE DO YOU FIND ANY REASON THAT SHE WOULD LIE ABOUT WHAT HAPPENED TO HER. RANDY LOOKED AT ANDREA AND SAID NO SHE WOULD NEVER LIE ABOUT SOMETHING LIKE THAT I HAD SEEN HOW SHE ALMOST KILLED HERSELF. HOW SHE WOULD CRY OUT FOR HELP AND THERE WAS NO ONE THERE TO ANSWER HER CRY HOW DO YOU SEE THE RELATIONSHIP BETWEEN HER AND HER PARENTS, RANDY LOOKED AT HER PARENTS AND SAID HATE AND TORTURE WHAT DO YOU MEAN HER DAD HATED ANDREA FOR NO REASON YES THAT IS WHAT I AM SAYING, AND HER MOM WAS NO BETTER THEY DID NOT LOVE HER OBJECTION YOUR HONOR HOW DO WE KNOW IF WHAT HE IS SAYING IS THE TRUTH OR IS NOT THE TRUTH ARGUMENTATIVE OVER RUDE. CONTIUE AS YOU WERE SAYING RANDY WHAT DO YOU MEAN BY SAYING HER MOM WAS NO BETTER HER MOM WOULD HIT HER FOR NO REASON, AND THEN THEY BOTH WOULD LAUGH AT HER AS SHE WAS THERE IN PAIN CRYING HOW LONG HAS THIS BEN GOING ON FOR, SHE WAS BEING ABUSE FOR 4 YEARS THANK YOU RANDY NO FURTHER QUESTIONS AS

THE ATTORNEY SITS DOWN THE JUDGE ASK THE ATTORNEY OF ANDREA PARENTS. WOULD YOU LIKE TO CROSS EXAMINE YES YOUR HONOR I WOULD AS HE WALKED TOWARDS RANDY AS RANDY WAS LOOKING AT ANDREA HE SAW SHE WAS IN TEARS, LOOKING AT WHAT WAS HAPPENING SO RANDY YOU ARE ANDREA BOYFRIEND YES I AM NOW HOW LONG HAVE YOU AND HER BEEN TOGETHE. FOR LIKE 7 YEARS THAT IS A LONG TIME SO HAVE YOU AND HER HAD INTIMATE LOVE OBJECTION YOUR HONOR SPECULATIVE LEADING THE WITNESS, THEIR REALTIONSHIP IS NOT ON TRAIL HERE SUSTAIN YOUR HONOR I AM TRYING TO PROVE A POINT, THAT ANDRAE WAS ALREADY ACTIVE SHE CLAIMS THAT HER DAD TOOK HER INNOCENT WHEN IT WAS ALREADY TAKEN BY RANDY SO WHAT HAPPENED TO HER DID NOT HAPPEN BY HER DAD. ORVERRULE CONTINUE WITH A NEW LINE OF QUESTIONS RANDY DID YOU EVER SEE ANDREA WITH OTHER BOYS, OBJECTION YOUR HONOR ARGUMENTATIVE SUSTAIN I GAVE YOU ONE WARNING TO MAINTAIN YOUR QUESTINS ABOUT THE MATTER AT HAND. RANDY DID YOU EVER SEE HER PARENS HIT HER OR DO ANY THING TO HER NO I DID NOT I NEVER WAS AT HER HOUSE WHEN ALL OF THIS WAS HAPPENING, SO YOU ARE SAYING YOU DO NOT KNOW WHAT HAPPENED HOW CAN YOU BELIEVE SOMETHING THAT YOU HAVE NEVER SEEN FOR YOURSELF, RANDY STAYED SILENT AND ASKED THE ATTORNEY CAN I ASK YOU A QUESTION YES WHAT IS IT, DO YOU HAVE KIDS YES I DO AND DO YOU BELIEVE IN THEM YES I DO SO IF YOUR SON CAME HOME AND SAID TO YOU I GOT IN A FIGHT IN SCHOL TODAY BUT YOU SAW NO BRUISE ON HIM WOULD YOU BELIEVE HIM. THE ATTORNEY STAYED SILENT FOR A BIT THEN HE SAID YES, I WOULD BELIEVE HIM HOW CAN YOU BELIEVE HIM IF YOU WERE NOT THERE TO SEE IT WITH YOUR OWN EYES HOW DO YOU KNOW IF YOUR SON WAS TELLING YOU THE TRUTH, CAUSE I KNOW MY SON DOES NOT LIE AND WOULD NOT LIE TO ME SO YOU SEE ANDREA HAS NEVER LIE TO ME BEFORE THAT IS WHY I BELIEVE HER, AFTER THE ATTORNEY SAID NO MORE QUESTIONS THE ATTORNEY WALKED AWAY THE JUDGE SAID YOU MAY STEP DOWN RANDY, AS RANDY WALKED BACK TO HIS SEAT HE WHISPERED TO ANDREA I LOVE YOU ANDREA JUST SMILED AND SAID I LOVE YOU TOO. THE JUDGE ASK ATTORNEY REYES TO CALL HIS NEXT WITNESS I CALL MR. GARCIA TO THE STAND AS ANDREA DAD WALKS TO THE STAND SHE GIVES HIM A LOOK OF HATRED, HE JUST LOOKS AT HER AND SMILE AS HE STANDS IN FRONT OF THE COURTROOM THE BAILIFF CAME TO SWEAR HIM IN DO YOU SWEAR TO TELL THE TRUTH THE WHOLE TRUTH AND NOTHING BUT THE TRUTH SO HELP YOU GOD, I DO YOU MAY BE SEATED MR. GARCIA ARE YOU ANDREA BIOLOGICAL FATHER HE STAYED SILENT FOR A MOMENT AS ANDREA LOOKED AT HIM WAITING FOR THE ANSWER THEN HE TOOK A DEEP BREATH AND

SAID NO I AM NOT HER REAL FATHER. BUT SHE IS MY BEAUTIFUL DAUGHTER I LOVE HER AND IS MRS. GARCIA HER BIOLOGICAL MOM AFTER HE ASKED THIS QUESTION AGAIN HE STAYED SILENT, AT THIS POINT ANDREA WAS ON THE EDGE OF HER SEAT AS HE LOOKED DOWN TO THE FLOOR THE JUDGE TURNED AND SAID TO ANSWER THE QUESTION, IS ANDREA MOTHER HER BIOLOGICL MOTHER HE CLEAR HIS THROAT AND SAID YES SHE IS AND SHE IS ALSO ANDREA OLDER SISTER. WHEN HE SAID THIS THE COURTROOM WAS IN SHOCK, THEY DID NOT KNOW WHAT TO BELIEVE AT THIS POINT EVERYONE WAS COUGHT OFF GUARD, THIS CASE WAS GETTING MORE EMOTIONAL ANDREA EYES FILLED UP WITH TEARS, SO HOW IS IT POSSIBLE THAT SHE IS ANDREAS OLDER SISTER WILL YOU SEE MY FIRST WIFE COULD NOT GIVE ME KIDS AND I WANTED A FAMILY SO I LEFT HER AND GOT MARRIED TO ANOTHER LADY, SHE GAVE ME A DAUGHTER WHICH WAS ANDREA'S OLDER SISTER AND AS SOON AS SHE WAS OLD ENOUGH I LEFT MY WIFE AND GOT TOGETHER WITH ANDREA OLDER SISTER. THE ATTONRNEY JUST STAND THERE SPEECHLESS WOW I NEVER HEARD OF SOMETHING SO DISTURBING AS YOU ARE TELLING ME, SO CONTINUE WHAT HAPPENED NEXT AND WHY DID YOU TURN LIKE THIS YOU SEE I WANTED MORE KIDS LATER ON IN LIFE BUT SHE DID NOT WANT NO MORE KIDS, SO I STAYED WITH HER A WHILE LONGER IT WAS GETTING CLOSE FOR ANGIE BIRTHDAY SHE WAS TURNING 15 YEARS OLD AND I CAME HOME ONE NIGHT AND MY WIFE HAD LEFT FOR A WHILE, I ACCIDENTALLY WALKED INTO ANGIE ROOM FORGETTING THAT SHE WAS MY DAUGHTER, AND JUST STOOD THERE AND LOOKED AT HER AND I SAW HER WITH NO CLOTHES ON I WALKED IN AND CLOSED THE DOOR AND SAID TO HER TONIGHT YOU WILL BE WITH ME. AND THAT NIGHT I GOT HER PREGNANT AFTER THAT DAY WE HAD NO CHOICE BUT TO STAY TOGETHER I LET MY WIFE GO AND ME AND ANGIE KEPT OUR TIME TOGETHER A SECRET AFTERWARDS A FEW YEARS LATER WHEN ANGIE TURNED 17 YEARS OLD I MARRIED HER, SO YES SHE IS ANDREA MOM WE NEVER MEANT TO HURT ANDREA IT ALL STARTED WHEN WE STARTED DOING DRUGS, THEN STARTED DOING OTHER BAD THINGS WHEN ANDREA TURNED 9 YEARS OLD THAT IS WHEN IT GOT WORSE, WE WERE SO LOST WITHOUT HOPE WE GOT INTO DRUGS DEEPER AND ALCOHOL WE WERE TRYING TO DROWN THE PAIN WE PUT PEOPLE THREW, WE FOUND OUR SELVES ALWAYS BROKE AND ALWAYS RUNNING OUT OF MONEY THEN ONE DAY I SAW ANDREA PLAYING, I WAS HAVING THOUGHTS OF BEING WITH HER AND IT SCARED ME TO BE THINKING LIKE THAT ABOUT MY 9 YEAR OLD DAUGHTER SO WHAT HAPPEN NEXT I TRY TO FORGET THOSES THOUGHTS BUT THEY KEPT COMING STRONGER AND STRONGER. DID YOU AND YOUR WIFE ABUSED ANDERA NO WE DID NOT WE TRIED TO DISCIPLIE HER AND TEACH HER RIGHT

FROM WRONG, WE WERE NOT THE BEST PARENTS WE TRIED TO BE GOOD PARENS OK MR. GARCIA NO FURTHER QUESTIONS MR. REYES WOULD YOU LIKE TO QUESTION THE DEFENDENT, YES YOUR HONOR AS THE ATTORNEY STOOD UP HE LOOKED AT ANDREA HE LOOKED AT HER PARENT WITHOUT A CARE IN THE WORLD, HE WAS SHOCKED AT HOW CAN THESES TO HAVE NO HEART FOR THEIR CHILD AS THE ATTORNEY WALKED TOWARD ANDREA'S DAD HE LOOKED CONFUSED AT HIM SHAKING HIS HEAD, IN CONFUSION I CAN NOT BELIEVE WHAT I HEARED WE KNOW THE TRUTH WAS ABOUT TO COME OUT. THE ATTORNEY WE HAVE IS A GREATE ATTORNEY OO MR. GARCIA YOU SAY YOU WERE TRYING TO DISCIPLINE AND SHOW ANDREA RIGHT FROM WRONG YES THAT IS RIGHT, WE TRY TO SHOW HER RIGHT FROM WRONG HOW CAN YOU TEACH A PEROSN TO BE GOOD IF YOU YOURSELF ARE NOT GOOD BUT EVIL, AND DON'T KNOW THE RIGHT FROM WRONG IF YOU DO NOT KNOW HOW TO LIVE YOUR LIFE RIGHT, SO TELL ME HOW IS THAT POSSIBLE YOU ARE HER DAD HOW COULD YOU EVEN THINK OF DONIG THS I AM SHOCKED AT WHAT YOU AND YOUR WIFE HAVE PUT HER THREW. I PROMISE YOU AND YOUR WIFE WILL NOT WALK OUT OF THIS COURTROOM, I HAVE NO MORE FOR THIS MONSTER EXCUSE ME I MEAN THIS PERSON YOU MAY STEP DOWN WE WILLL BREAK FOR LUNCH COURT WILL RESUME AT 3 O'CLOCK, THE ATTORNEY SAID LET'S GO WE GOT UP AN LEFT THE COURTROOM ANDREA WAS STARTING TO SEE THE LIGHT AS SHE KNEW IN HER HEART IT WOULD BE JUST A MATTER OF TIME BEFORE IT WOULD ALL END, JUDY WOULD YOU LIKE TO JOIN US FOR LUNCH WE NEED TO GO OVER LOT'S OF SUFF. WE HAVE LITTLE TIME THERE IS ALOT WE HAVE TO GO OVER TO GET YOU READY TO TESTIFY, JUDY IS COMING WITH US SO WE NEED TO TALK AND FILL YOU AND YOUR PARENTS IN ON WHAT IS GOING ON SO FAR YES MY PARENTS SAID IT IS FINE WE CAN ALL GO FOR LUNCH, OK JUDY AS I SAID I WILL BE CALLING YOU TO THE STAND NEXT SO YOU THINK IT IS THE RIGHT TIME FOR ME TO GO ON THE STAND, YES IT IS THE PERFECT TIME FOR YOU TO TAKE THE STAND WE HAVE THEM AT THE PONT WE WANT THEM AND YOUR TESTIMONY WILL FOR SURE PUT THEM AWAY FOR GOOD. THE DAD IS CLAIMING HE IS A GREAT PERSON WE ARE GOING TO PROVE THAT HE IS NOTHING BUT LIES AND HE WILL LOOSE ALL CREDIBILITY WITH THE JURY, OK THEN I AM READY FOR WHAT I MUST DO TO PREPARE FOR THIS I WILL DO ANYHING FOR ANDREA I WILL RUN YOU THREW YOUR DEFENSE, ANDREA AND RANDY GET A TABLE AND LET ME TALK TO JUDY AND FILL HER IN ON EVERYTHNG SHE NEEDS TO KNOW SINCE SHE WAS NOT THERE FOR THE TRAIL YESTERDAY. JUDY LET SIT HERE AT THIS TABLE OK I CALLED RANDY TO TESTIFY FIRST AND RANDY MADE THE OTHER ATTORNEY LOOK REALLY STUPID, THEN THEY CALLED ANDREA DAD AND HE GOT

PUT TO SHAME HE TRIED TO TALK HIS WAY OUT AND PLAY THE NOBLE PERSON MR. GOOD FATHER, BUT THE JURY DID NOT BELIEVE IT AND EVERYTHING WENT OUR WAY YESTERDAY AND NOW WITH YOUR TESTIMONY THEY WILL LOSE EVERYTHING AND GET SENT AWAY. AS THE ATTORNEY AND JUDY RETURN BACK TO SIT WITH ANDREA AND RANDY THEY LOOK HAPPY OK ANDREA JUDY IS READY YES I AM READY TO TAKE THE STAND TOMORROW, LET'S START GOING BACK TO THE COURTHOUSE WHEY WILL NOT SEE WHAT IS ABOUT TO HAPPEN, THEY HAVE NO CLUE AND THEY WILL BE SURPRISED AS WE GOT TO THE COURTHOUSE ANDRA LOOKED UP AND WAS COUGHT BY SURPRISE HER AUNT AND GRANDMA WAS THERE, ON THE STRPS WAITING FOR ANDREA TO SHOW UP GRANDMA WHAT ARE YOU AND SUSAN DOING HERE, WE KNEW WE NEEDED TO BE HERE WITH YOU AND STAND BY YOUR SIDE AND SUPPORT YOU I LOVE YOU GRANDMA AND AUNT SUSIE. GRANDMA THIS MY BOYFRIEND RANDY AND RANDY THIS IS MY VERY BEAUTIFUL GRANDMA AND MY AUNT SUSIE, THEY WERE THE ONES I WAS STAYING WITH GRANDMA RANDY WILL BE GOING BACK WITH ME, TO STAY WITH YOU WILL RANDY WE ARE VERY HAPPY TO FINALLY MEET YOU AND ANDREA HAS TOLD US SO MUCH ABOUT YOU. AND WE FEEL THAT WE HAVE KNOWN YOU FOR A VERY LONG TIME, WELCOME TO THE FAMILY THANK YOU MRS GARCIA, I LOVE ANDREA VERY MUCH WILL LET'S GO INSIDE THE COURTROOM. MOM AND DAD WILL BE SURPRISED TO SEE THE BOTH OF YOU YES I BET THEY WILL BE HOW IS THE CASE GOING FROM THE WAY THINGS LOOK IT IS GOING VERY WELL, AND IT IS FIXING TO GET VERY INTERESTING WHAT DO YOU MEAN YOU WILL SEE GRANMA AS WE WALK INTO THE COURTROOM ANDREA PARENTS LOOKED AT ANDREA GRANDMA AND AUNT WITH A LOOK OF CONFUSION AND FEAR, FOR SOME REASON ANDERA PARENTS WERE SCARE OF HRE GANDMA AND AUNT AS THEY SAT DOWN ANDREA DAD ASK WHAT ARE YOU BOTH DOING HERE, LEAVE YOU BOTH NEED TO LEAVE WE ARE HERE TO SEE YOU BOTH GET WHAT YOU BOTH DESERVE. FOR HURTING THIS POOR GIRL SO SON THIS IS ONE PLACE YOU CAN NOT KICK US OUT OF SO SIT THERE WITH YOUR DAUGHTER, AND TAKE YOUR PAIN AND SUFFERING AND GET YOUR PUSNISHMENT AS YOU BOTH GAVE IT OUT SO FREELY, AND YOU BOTH WILL FEEL THE PAIN AND SUFFERING ANDREA WENT THROUGH IN YOUR HANDS. I STILL DO NOT UNDERSTAND HOW THE BOTH OF YOU CAN DO THIS TO YOUR DAUGHTER, ALL SHE WANTED WAS A CHANCE TO FEEL LOVE AND HAPPINESSS BUT THANKS TO THE BOTH OF YOU HER LIFE IS NOW DESTROYED FROM THE INSIDE OUT. REMEMBER THIS DAY AND MARK MY WORDS YOU BOTH WILL GET WHAT YOU DESERVE WHEN YOU GO TO PRISON REMEMBER THEY HATE PEOPLE LIKE YALL, IN THERE AND NO ONE WILL HELP YOU OUT I SHOULD BE MAD AT THE

BOTH OF YALL BUT I FEEL SORRY FOR YOU AND YOUR DAUGHTER FOR THE PAIN AND SUFFERING THE BOTH OF YOU ARE GOING TO EXPERIENCE, I WISH THIS ON NO ONE NOT EVEN MY WORST ENEMIE. BUT YOU SHOULD KNOW THAT THE UGLY YOU PUT OUT INTO THE WORLD COMES BACK TO YOU TWICE AS BAD, AND NOW THE REALITY OF WHAT YOU DID AND THE TRUEL EVIL PEOPLE YOU BOTH ARE WILL BE BROUGHT TO LIGHT I WILL PRAY FOR YOU BOTH, AS ANDREA GRANDMA TELLS HER DAD THIS HE HAS NOTHING TO SAY HE JUST SITS THERE SPEECHLES AS IF HE IS LOST AT THE FACT THAT HIS LIFE WILL SOON BE OVER AND THERE IS NOTHING THAT NO ONE CAN DO.

CHAPTER 8   PRAYERS BEEN ANSWERED

OR WILL DO TO HELP YOU AS YOU BOTH LAUGH AT ANDREA PAIN AND SUFFERING FOR SO MANY YEARS THEY WILL ALSO LAUGH AT YOUR PAIN THEY WILL HAVE THEIR WAY WITH YOU AND YOUR WFE, SO GET READY FOR THE BEGINNING OF THE END OF YOUR SO -CALLED DISGUSTING LIFE MAY GOD HELP YOU CAUSE NO ONE ELSE WILL, AFTER ANDREA AUNT TOLD HER PARENTS THIS SHE JUST SAT THERE WITH A LOOK OF HATRED TOWARD THE BOTH OF THEM, AT THIS POINT THE JUDGE WAS WALKING IN ALL RISE THE HONORABLE JUDGE WRIGHT PRESIDING YOU MAY BE SEATED MR. REYES CALL YOUR FIRST WINESS I CALL JUDY RAMIREZ TO THE STAND AS SHE WAS CALLED ANDREA'S PARENTS ATTORNEY SPOKE OBJECTION YOUR HONOR, WE KNOW NOTHING ABOUT THIS WITNESS I HAVE NOT HAD THE TIME TO GO OVER HER FILE AND SEE HOW SHE IS RELATED TO THIS TRIAL. OVER RUDE I AM ALLOWING THIS WITNESS JUDY DO YOU SWEAR TO TELL THE TRUTH THE WHOLE TRUTH AND NOTHING BUT THE TRUTH SO HELP YOU GOD YES I DO, YOU MAY BE SEATED AS THE ATTORNEY WALKS TOWARDS JUDY SHE IS FILLED WITH TEARS AND FEAR IN HER EYES AS SHE LOOKS AT ANDREAS DAD WHY ARE YOU CRYING AND SHE WHISPERS I AM SCARD, SCARE OF WHAT I AM SCARED OF THAT DIRTY MAN AND LADY THERE LOOK AT ME JUDY I PROMISE YOU THAT YOU ARE SAFE THEY CAN NOT HURT YOU NO MORE. TELL THE COURT EVERYTHING THAT HAPPENED NOW JUDY DO YOU KNOW ANDREA NO I DON'T TELL ME IN YOUR OWN WORDS WHY ARE YOU HERE TODAY, AND WHAT HAPPENED TO YOU, WILL IT HAPPEN LIKE THIS LAST YEAR I WAS A THE PLAY GOUND IN FRONT OF MY HOUSE AND THESE TWO PEOPLE CALLED ME TO THEIR CAR ASKING IF I HAD SEEN THEIR DOG, I

SAID NO I HAVE NOT AS SOON AS I TURNED TO WALK AWAY THE MAN GOT OUT OF THE CAR AND FORCED ME TO GET INTO THERE CAR, WITH THEM THE LADY LAUGHED AND SAID SINCE OUR DAUGHTER IS NOT HERE YOUR GOING TO TAKE HER PLACE AND MAKE MONEY FOR US AT FIRST I DID NOT KNOW WHAT THEY WERE TALKING ABOUT. WHEN WE GOT TO THEIR HOUSE I WAS BLINDFOLDED THEY TOOK ME INTO WHAT I BELIEVE TO HAD BEEN ANDREA ROOM THEY MADE ME SHOWER AND PUT ON ANDREA CLOTHES, THEN WHEN I WAS DONE IT STARTED WHAT STARTED JUDY WHAT HAPPENED TELL US AS JUDY SAT ON THE WITNESS CHAIR SHE WAS FULL OF TEARS AND THEN SHE SPOKE THEY TOOK ME TO THE BED. AND THE MAN SAID I GOTTA SEE HOW GOOD YOU ARE I TOLD HIM NO DO NOT DO THAT TO ME I PLEADED WITH HIM BUT HE WOULD NOT STOP, I YELLED FOR HELP NO ONE HEARD ME MOMMY I TOLD HIM TO STOP HURTING ME WHY DID HE NOT LISTEN THEY JUST LAUGH AT ME, HOW OLD WERE YOU WHEN THIS HAPPENED I WAS ONLY 12 YEARS OLD BUT THAT IS NOT THE WORST PART, WHAT WAS THE WORST PART WILL IT WAS WHEN HE STARTED CALLING HIS FRIENDS AND THEY TOOK TURNS ON ME, SLAPPING ME AND CALLING ME ALL KINDS OF NAMES I HAVE NO FURTHER QUESTIONS. ATTORNEY SANCHEZ WOULD YOU LIKE TO CROSS EXAMINE NO QUESTIONS YOUR HONOR YOU CAN STEP DOWN, YOU WERE BRAVE WE WILL PICK UP TOMORROW COURT ADJOURN ALL RISE AS THE JUDGE LEAVES THE ROOM YALL ARE FREE TO LEAVE, AS ANDREA AND EVERYONE WALKED OUT ANDREA WENT UP TO JUDY GAVE HER A BIG HUG, AND TOLD HER I KNOW IT WAS HARD TO TALK ABUOT IT I JUST HOPE I AM AS STRONG AS YOU WERE WHEN I AM CALLED TO THE STAND. AS ANDREA SAID THAT THE ATTORNEY CAME UP TO HER WE ARE GOING TO FIND OUT TOMORROW, YOU WILL BE CALLED TO THE STAND BE READY YOUR TESTIMONY IS THE MOST IMPORTANT ONE. ANDREA THIS IS THE MOMENT YOU BEEN WAITING FOR ALL OF YOUR LIFE NOW IT IS YOUR TIME TO SHINE AS ANDREA STANDS THERE SILENT, RANDY SAY'S TO HER MY LOVE YOUR DAY HAS FINALLY ARRIVED AND I KNOW YOU WILL DO GREAT ON THAT STAND AS THE DAY CAME TO AN END ALL ANDREA COULD DO WAS THINK ABOUT THE DAY TO COME, SHE STAYED UP MOST OF THE NIGHT LOCKED HERSELF IN HER ROOM DID NOT WANT TO BE BOTHERED BY NO ONE. RANDY KNOCKED ON THE DOOR ASKING HER IS SHE WAS HUNGRY SHE RESPONDED NO I AM OK I JUST WANT TO BE LEFT ALONE I HAVE A LOT TO THINK ABOUT, I NEED TO BE READY FOR TOMORROW AS RANDY WALKED AWAY FROM THE DOOR ALL HE COULD DO WAS THINK ABOUT ANDREA HOW EVERYTHING HAS BEEN GOING, AND HOW EMOTIONAL THE TRAIL HAS BEEN AND STARTING TOMORROW IT IS GOING TO BE MORE HEART BREAKNG. ANDREA IS GOING TO LET THE WHOLE WORLD KNOW EVERYTHING

THAT HER PARENTS AND THOSE MEN DID TO HER. RANDY JUST SAT AT THE TABLE AND TEARS FELL FROM HIS EYES THEY WERE THE KIND OF TEARS THAT NO ONE CAN EXPLAIN, SO MANY EMOTIONS WERE RACING THREW HIS HEAD AND HE NEVER THOUGHT THAT HE WOULD BE INVOLVED IN A RELATIONSHIP LIKE THIS AS RANDY CLOSE HIS EYES HE FALLS INTO A DEEP SLEEP, MORNING IS NEAR AS ANDREA LOOKS OUT THE WINDOW SHE MAKES A WISH UPON THE BRIGHTEST STAR WISHING THAT ALL OF THIS WILL SOON BE OVER, THE ATTORNEY SPENT THE REST OF THE NIGHT PREPARING THE LETTERS FOR TOMORROW TRAIL THESE LETTERS ARE A VITAL PART OF THE TRAIL. AND THE ONE THAT IS GOING TO HURT MORE THAN ANYONE ELSE IS ANDREA AS SHE READ'S THE LETTERS SHE MUST EXPLAIN IN DETAIL EXACTLY WHAT HAPPENED THE NIGHT'S AT QUESTION IN THE LETTERS. FINALLY AT MIDNIGHT THE ATTORNEY FELL ASLEEP THE WHOLE WORLD SLEPT ONLY ANDREA COULD NOT SLEEP ALL NIGHT, SHE JUST TOSSED AND TURNED MORNING HAS ARRIVED LET'S LOOK ON AS ANDREA AND RANDY PREPARE TO GO TO THE COURTHOUSE ANDREA RECIVED A PHONE CALL, RANDY ANSWERED THE PHONE HELLO WHO IS SPEAKING HELLO RANDY IT IS ME JUDY HI JUDY GOOD MORNING. YES MAY I SPEAK TO ANDREA YES HOLD ON AS RANDY YEALLS OUT TO ANDREA IT IS FOR YOU JUDY IS CALLING YOU OK TELL HER GIVE ME A SECOND I AM GETTING READY, JUDY ANDREA SAID GIVE HER A SECOND SHE IS GETTING READY OH WAIT HER SHE COMES HELLO JUDY WHATS UP WILL IT IS MY DAD WHAT'S GONG ON WITH YOUR DAD, I OVERHEARD HIM LAST NIGHT TALKING TO MY MOM SAYING HE WAS GOING TO KILL YOUR DAD OH NO JUDY YOU AND YOUR MOM NEED TO STOP HIM, WE DO NOT NEED HIM GETTING IN TROUBLE THE LAW IS HANDLING THE CASE I KNOW WE TRIED TALKING TO HIM BUT HE IS NOT LISTENING TO US. I WILL KEEP A CLOSE EYE ON HIM AND MAKE SURE HE DOES NOT DO NOTHING CRAZY OK THANKS SEE YALL AT THE COURTHOUSE AS RANDY WALKS IN AND SAW ANDREA, HE ASK HER WHAT WAS WRONG IT IS JUDY DAD HE WANTS TO KILL MY DAD FOR WHAT HE DID TO HER NO HE CAN'T DO THAT I WILLL KEEP AN EYE ON HIM, MAKING SURE HE DOES NOT THROW HIS LIFE AWAY THANKS RANDY WE DO NOT NEED TO BE GOING TO A MURDER TRAIL. ARE YOU READY YES I AM LET'S GO, I AM SURE THE ATTORNEY IS WAITING FOR US AT THE COURTHOUSE AS WE LEFT ALL WE COULD DO WAS JUST THINK ABOUT WHAT JUDY TOLD ME, ABOUT HERE DAD THIS WAS GOING TO BE A VERY INTERESTING DAY WE ARE ALREADY 2 MONTHS INTO THE TRAIL IT IS GOING IN OUR FAVOR WE DO NOT NEED THIS INTERFERENCE, RANDY DO YOU THINK WE SHOULD TELL THE ATTORNEY WHAT JUDY TOLD ME YES YOU NEED TO TELL HIM BECAUSE IF YOU DON'T THEN IF HE DOES KILL HIM AND WE DID NOT SAY ANYTHING WE

CAN BE CHARGED AS ACCOMPLISHED TO THE MURDER, AND YOUR CASE WILL BE LOST YES YOU ARE RIGHT WE MUST TELL THE ATTORNEY AS WE GET TO THE COURTHOUSE. WE SEE THE ATTORNEY AT THE FRONT DOOR LOOKING AT SOME PAPERS GOOD MORNING MR REYES GOOD MORNING ANDREA AND RANDY LOOK MR. REYES I NEED TO TELL YOU SOMETHING VERY IMPORANT, WHAT IS GOING ON COME LET'S SIT HERE NOW TELL ME I TALK TO JUDY THIS MORNING SHE TOLD ME THAT HER DAD SAID HE WAS GOING TO KILL MY DAD, HE WAS VERY MAD AND HURT AT THE FACT OF WHAT MY DAD DID TO JUDY OH NO WE CAN NOT ALLOW THAT I WILL LET THE COURT POLICE KNOW AND THEY WILL STAND GUARD TO MAKE SURE THIS DOES NOT HAPPEN. ANDREA ARE YOU READY TO GO IN THIS IS YOUR BIG DAY YES I AM READY LET'S DO THIS AS WE START WALKING IN WE SEE JUDY AND HER PARENTS INSIDE ALREADY, I WENT TO TALK TO JUDY AND I TOLD HER THAT THE ATTORNEY KNEW HER DAD'S PLANS TO KILL MY DAD NOW I KNOW HE DESERVES IT WE HAVE TO LET JUSTICE BE SERVED THE RIGHT WAY JUDY AND RANDY SAT BEHIND ANDREA, AS ANDREA AND ATTORNEY REYES TOOK THEIR SEAT IN FRONT OF THE JUDGE ALL RISE COURT IN SESSION THE HONORABLE JUDGE WRIGHT PRESIDING ALL MAY BE SEATED, GOOD MORNING COURT MR REYES CALL YOUR FIRST WITNESS I CALL ANDREA GARCIA TO THE STAND ANDREA RAISE YOUR HAND, DO YOU SWEAR TO TELL THE TRUTH THE WHOLE TRUTH AND NOTHING BUT THE TRUTH SO HELP YOU GOD YES I DO YOU MAY BE SEATED. AS ANDREA SIT'S AT THE WITNESS CHAIR THE COURTROOM DOOR OPENS SLOWLY ANDREA AND EVERYONE LOOKED TO SEE WHO WAS COMING IN, IT WAS JUDY'S DAD HE WALKS IN AND GOES STRAIGHT TO ANDREA DAD AND PULLS OUT A GUN AND HE SAYS TO HIM YOU WILL NEVER HURT ANOTHER CHILD, BEFORE HE HAD A CHANCE TO PULL THE TRIGGER ANDREA YELLED AS LOUD AS SHE CULD NO STOP DO NOT KILL HIM PLEASE JUSTICE WILL BE SERVED FOR YOUR DAUGHTER. AND ME AND ALL THE KIDS HE HURT DO IT FOR US BUT MOST OF ALL DO IT FOR YOUR DAUGHTER SHE NEEDS YOU HERE WITH HER NOT IN PRISON, PLEASE DON'T TRADE PLACES WITH HIM AS ANDREA SAID THIS JUDY'S DAD DROPPED THE GUN AND DROPPED TO HIS KNEES IN TEARS AND SAID YOUR RIGHT I AM SORRY, AS THE COPS WERE TAKING HIM AWAY THE JUDGE SPOKE NO LET HIM GO SIR YOU MAY TAKE YOUR SEAT THANK YOU YOUR HONOR. JUDY GOT UP FROM HER SEAT WALKED TOWARDS HER DAD GRABBED HIS HAND AND SAID COME ON DAD LET'S GO SIT DOWN, AS ANDREA SAID JUSTICE WILL BE SERVE AS THEY WERE SITTING DOWN ATTORNEY REYES STARTED TALKING TO ANDREA CAN YOU STATE YOUR NAME FOR THE COURT, MY NAME IS ANDREA GARCIA, ANDREA DID YOUR PARENTS ABUSE YOU OBEJECTION YOUR HONOR LEADING THE WITNESS SUSTAIN MR.

REYES PLEASE CLEARIFY YOUR QUESTION, YES YOUR HONOR ANDREA CAN YOU TELL THE COURT WHY YOU ARE HERE TODAY I AM HERE TO GET JUSTICE MAY I ASK JUSTICE FOR WHAT, PLEASE BE SPECIFIC JUSTICE FOR THE ABUSE AND ASSAULT MY PARENTS PUT ME THREW SINCE I WAS 9 YEARS OLD ANDREA I HAVE HERE IN MY HANDS THE LETTERS THAT YOU WROTE TO ROBERT, I AM GOING TO GIVE YOU THE LETTERS ONE AT A TIME AND PLEASE EXPLAIN WHAT HAPPEN ON THOSE DAYS IN QUESTION,OJECTION YOUR HONOR HOW DO WE KNOW THOSE LETTERS ARE TRUE AND IF THAT REALLY HAPPEN AS IT IS WRITTEN IN THE LETTERS YOUR HONOR I ALSO HAVE THE MEDICAL RECORDS FROM THE HOSPITAL, THAT WILL BACK UP THIS TESTIMONY OF THESES LETTERS ALL THE FACTS ARE HERE OVERRULE BEGAN MR. REYES YES YOUR HONOR ANDREA ARE YOU READY FOR THE FIRST LETTER. YES, I AM ANDREA HAND WAS SHAKING AS TH ATTORNEY WAS GIVEING HER THE LETTER AS SHE GRABBED THE LETTER IN HER HAND ANDREA STAYED QUIET, FOR A FEW SECONDS THEN SHE OPENED THE LETTER AS SOON AS SHE SAW THE WORDS ON THAT LETTER TEARS FLOWED FROM HER EYES. THE ATTORNEY ASKED ANDREA TO EXPLAIN THE LETTER SHE WROTE OK THIS LETTER IS DATED OCTOBER 12, 1977 AND IT READS AS FOLLOW HELLO ROBERT HOW ARE YOU DOING, AS FOR ME I DON'T KNOW I AM IN PAIN DOWN THERE MY DADDY WAS PLAYING WITH ME ROUGH HE SAID WE ARE GOING TO PLAY A GAME THAT DADDY AND DAUGHTERS PLAY, IT IS OUR GAME OUR SECREAT DON'T TELL NO ONE SO I SAID OK DADDY I WON'T TELL WE ARE GOING TO PLAY HOUSE. AND YOU ARE MY PRETEND WIFE YOU WILL HAVE FUN IN THE GAME OK DADDY HOW YOU PLAY THE FIRST THING A WIFE DOES IS MAKE HER HUSBAND HAPPY. YOU WANT TO MAKE DADDY HAPPY RIGHT YES DADDY OK DO WHAT DADDY SAY'S AND YOU WILL MAKE ME HAPPY THEN HE GOT ON TOP OF ME AND HE HURT ME, I SAW SOMETHING RED AND IT HURTS TO WALK I TOLD HIM TO STOP I DID NOT WANT TO PLAY NO MORE AND HE LAUGH AND SAID DADDY IS HAVING FUN, WHY DID DADDY HURT ME TALK TO YOU TOMORROW THIS IS THE FIRST LETTER I WROTE TO ROBERT ANDERA IN YOUR OWN WORDS TELL US EXACTLY HOW AND WHAT HAPPEND. THAT DAY WILL I WAS IN THE KITCHEN WITH MOM AND HE HAD JUST GOT HOME FROM WORK HE CAME TO ME AND PICKED ME UP AND KISSED ME ON MY LIPS AND SQUEEZED MY BOTTOM, LATER ON THAT NIGHT WHEN MY MOM WENT TO SLEEP THAT IS WHEN THE WORST DAY OF MY LIFE STARTED WHAT STARTED ANDREA PLEASE TELL THE COURT, ANDREA STAYED SILENT LOOKING DOWN THEN PUT HER HANDS OVER HER FACE WITH TEARS FALLING SHE LOOKED UP AND SAID THAT MONSTER CAME INTO MY ROOM AND ABUSED ME I WAS ONLY 10 YEARS OLD, AS ANDREA LOOKED AT HER PARENTS SHE ASK HOW COULD YOU BOTH DO THIS

TO ME I WAS JUST A KID 10 YEARS OLD YOU BOTH ARE EVIL PEOPLE, AND YOU BOTH WILL GET WHAT YOU DESERVE I HAVE NO FURTHER QUESTIONS MR. SANCHEZ WOULD YOU LIKE TO CROSS EXAMINE YES YOUR HONOR I WOULD THE ATTORNEY TOOK A MOMENT TO GET UP, AS THE JUDGE ASK HIM AGAIN MR. SANCHEZ WOULD YOU LIKE TO QUESTION THE WITNESS YES YOUR HONOR AS HE GET'S UP TO GO QUESTION ANDREA HE IS SMIRKING, WOW I HEARD SOME STORIES IN THE PASS BUT THIS IS THE BEST WHY WOULD YOUR DAD DO THAT TO YOU HIS DAUGHTER YOU HAVE AN IMAGINATION. HOW MANY MORE STORIES ARE YOU GOING TO TELL? OBJECTION YOUR HONOR SPECULATION IS THEIR A QUESTION HERE SUSTAIN, MR. SANCHEZ WHAT IS THE QUESTION ANDREA IS IT TRUE THAT YOU WERE ALWAYS GETTING IN TROUBLE AS YOU WERE GROWING UP AND YOUR PARENTS TRY TO GIVE YOU A GOOD LIFE, AND ACTUALLY YOU ARE THE ONE THAT REJECTED THEM AFTER EVRYTHING THEY DID FOR YOU THE WAY YOU PAY THEM BACK IS BY TRYING TO HAVE THEM SENT TO PRISON, FOR THE REST OF THEIR LIFE NO YOU ARE WRONG MR.SANCHEZ YOU WERE NOT THERE WHEN ALL OF THIS WAS HAPPENING TO ME. YOU WERE NOT THERE WHEN I WOULD WAKE UP AT NIGHT IN A DEEP SWEAT CRYING AND HUGGING MY PILLOW SCARED EVERY TIME THE DOOR OPENED, THINKING IT WAS MY DAD OR MY MOM OR ANOTHER MAN COMING IN TO TAKE ADVANTAGE OF ME, OR START HITTING, ME SO DON'T SIT THERE IN YOUR THRIFT STORE SUIT THINKING YOU KNOW EVERYTHING WHEN YOU KNOW NOTHING THE ONLY THINKG YOU KNOW IS WHAT THOSE TWO MONSTERS TOLD YOU. AS ANDREA SAID THIS THE WHOLE COURT ROOM WAS QUITE THEN ANDERA LOOK AT THE ATTORNEY AND SAID I ASSURE YOU THAT YOU WILL SEE THE TRUTH, ABOUT THESE TWO PEOPLE AS WE ARE HERE FOR THE TRUTH IS COMING OUT THEN THE ATTORNEY SAID I HAVE NO MORE QUESTIONS YOU MAY STEP DOWN, AS ANDREA WALKED BACK TO HER SEAT SHE LOOKED AT HER PARENTS WITH SO MUCH HATE ANDREA YOU DID A GREAT JOB ON THAT STAND, NOW I MIGHT BE CALLING YOU BACK TO THE STAND LATER ON I AM READY FOR ALL OF THIS TO BE OVER WITH HOW MUCH LONGER IS ALL OF THIS GOING TO LAST. WILL THE WAY IT LOOKS I FEEL IT WILL BE OVER SOONER THEN YOU THINK JUST KEEP YOUR HEAD UP AND YOU WILL SEE ALL WILL COME TO PASS MY LOVE YOU WERE WONDRFUL UP THERE, I KNOW IT WAS HARD FOR YOU TO TALK ABOUT YOUR PASS AND WHEN THIS IS OVER YOU WILL NEVER HAVE TO DEAL WTIH THEM AGAIN, MY LOVE SOON IT WILL BE OVER I PROMISE AS RANDY SPOKE TO ANDREA ALL SHE COULD DO WAS THINK THAT IT WOULD ALL BE OVER SOON. AS ANDREA GRABBED HER SEAT THE JUDGE SAID MR SANCHEZ CALL YOUR FIRST WITNESS I CALL MRS. GARCIA AS ANDREA MOM GET'S UP TO TAKE THE STAND SHE LOOKS TOWARD ANDRA AND

JUST SMILES, DO YOU SWEAR TO TELL THE TRUTH THE WHOLE TRUTH AND NOTHING BUT THE TRUTH SO HELP YOU GOD I DO YOU MAY BE SEATED, MRS. GARCIA CAN YOU TELL THE COURT IN YOUR OWN WORDS EVERYTHING THAT WENT ON IN YOUR HOUSE EVERY DETAIL WILL THE LIES STARTED WHEN SHE WAS ABOUT 9 YEARS OLD WHEN SHE DID NOT GEET HER WAY. SHE WOULD LIE AND SAY THAT WE ABUSED HER THE LIES CONTINUED ALL HER LIFE WE TRIED TO BE GOOD PARENTS BUT HOW CAN YOU BE GOOD PARENTS TO A CHILD WHO IS REBELLIOUS TOWARDS HER PARENTS. AND NOT WANTING TO DO AS WE ASK HER, WE WERE GOOD TO OUR CHILD ANDREA AND WE DO NOT UNDERSTAND WHY SHE IS DOING THIS TO US, I KNOW IT IS THAT BOY THAT SHE IS WITH WHO IS PUTTING HER UP TO THIS SHE WAS A GOOD GIRL UNTIL SHE MET HIM, OBJECTION YOUR HONOR SPECULATIVE IT IS HER OWN OPINION THERE IS NO EVIDENCE TO BACK UP HER STATEMENT OVER RULE MR. SANCHEZ WARNED YOUR CLIENT TO STICK TO THE FACTS, YES YOUR HONOR SO MRS. GARCIA WHEN DID YOU NOTICE A CHANGE IN ANDREA ATTITUDE I NOTICE THAT THE FOLLOWING DAY AFTER I LET HER GO STAY THE NIGHT AT HER FRIENDS HOUSE, SHE STARTED ACTING UP THANK YOU MRS. GARCIA NO FURTHER QUESTINS MR. REYES WOULD YOU LIKE TO CROSS EXAMIN YES I WOULD YOUR HONOR MRS. GARCIA YOU STATED THAT ANDREA ATTITUDE CHANGED DO YOU REMEMBER EXACTLY WHAT DAY THAT WAS AND REMEMBER YOUR UNDER OATH NO I DO NOT RECALL IT HAS BEEN SUCH A LONG TIME AGO, YOU KNOW MRS. GARCIA THAT IS THE GOOD THING ABOUT RECORDS THEY KEEP TRACK OF THINGS THT HAPPENS YEARS AGO SO I HAVE THE RECORDS HERE IN MY HAND, NOW LET ME REFRESH YOUR MEMORY IT WAS OCTOBER 12 1977 DOES THAT RING A BELL ANDREA MOM STAYED SILENT MRS. GARCIA ANSWER THE QUESTION. YES I REMEMBER THAT DAY YES TELL US WHAT HAPPEN THAT DAY IT WAS THE FIRST DAY MY HUSBAND ABUSE HER YES THAT IS RIGHT, IT WAS THE FIRST TIME YOUR HUSBAND ABUSE HER THAT IS WHY SHE WANTED TO LEAVE SHE NEEDED TO GO TO THE HOSPITAL AND INSTEAD OF HELPING HER YALL ABUSED HER, WILL SHE DID GO TO THE HOSPITAL HER FRIENDS MOM TOOK HER AND I HAVE THE DR. REPORT HERE IN MY HAND SHOULD I READ IT TO THE COURT. OR ARE YOU GOING TO COME CLEAN AND TELL US THE TRUTH OK I WILL READ THE REPORT MEDICAL RECORDS FOR ANDRA GARCIA, DATED OCTOBER 12 1977 ANDREA WAS ADMITTED TO THE HOSPITAL AND SEEN BY DR. MORALES ANDREA COMPLAINED OF INTERNAL PAIN IN HER STOMACH AND HER PRIVATE PART AFTER FURTHER TEST ANDREA WAS DIAGNOSED, AND THE RESULT OF THE EXAMINATION THAT ANDREA SUFFERED FROM BEING MOLESTED BY A FAMILY MEMBER OBJECTION YOUR HONOR IS MR. REYES SPEAKING FACTS, OR IS HE

ASSUMING THAT WAS THE MEDICAL CAUSE YOUR HONOR I HAVE THE HOSPITAL REPORT HERE IN MY HAND OVER RULED THE COURT WILL ALLOW IT AS EVIDENCE, NOW MRS. GARCIA YOU KNEW WHAT HAPPENED THAT NIGHT AND INSTEAD OF HELPING YOUR CHILD YOU TRY TO COVER UP FOR YOUR HUSBAND, AS MRS GARCIA SITS THERE SHE HAS NOTHING TO SAY THEN THE ATTORNEY SAYS I HAVE NO FURTHER QUESTIONS YOU MAY STEP DOWN, MRS. GARCIA AS ANDREA MOM STEPS DOWN EVERYONE WAS JUST LOOKING AT HER WITH SO MUCH HATE. THEN THE JUDGE SAID MR. REYES CALL YOUR NEXT WITNESS YOUR HONOR MY WITNESS HAS NOT MADE IT HERE CAN WE GET A CONTINUES THE COURT ADJOURNED, TIL 9 IN THE MORNING ALL RISE A THE HONORABLE JUDGE LEAVES THE COURTROOM AS THE JUDGE LEAVES THE COPS SAYS COURT IS DISMISSED YOU ALL MAY LEAVE, AS EVERYONE WALKS OUT OF THE COURTROOM RANDY STAYS QUIET ANDREA LOOKED AT RANDY SAYING RANDY WHAT IS ON YOUR MIND, YOU HAVE NOT SAID ANYTHING ALL DAY WHAT ARE THNKING ABOUT I AM THINKING ABOUT YOUR BROTHER WHAT ABOUT MY BROTHER WHEN WAS THE LAST TIME YOU SEEN HIM, THE LAST TIME I SAW HIM I WAS ONLY 9 YEARS OLD SO HE IS ABOUT 13 YEARS OLD RIGHT NOW I WISH I COULD SEE HIM. NO TELLING WHERE HE IS ONLY GOD KNOWS MY LOVE LET'S PRAY THAT HE RETURNS SOON, AS FOR NOW WE NEED TO MEET UP WITH THE ATTORNEY ALL WE COULD DO WAS THINK ABOUT WHERE ANDERA BROTHER WAS AND HOW HE WAS DOING MR. REYES WHAT IS THE PLAN FOR TOMORROW. YOU KNOW WE HAVE BEEN GOING TO COURT FOR THE MATTER AT HAND FOR ALMOST A YEAR WILL ANDREA TOMORROW COULD BE THE LAST DAY IF THINGS GO AS PLANNED, SO TOMORROW WE LAY EVRYTHING ON THE TABLE THE TRAIL IS GOING IN OUR FAVOR YOU HAVE NOTHING TO WORRY ABOUT ANDREA YOU HAVE THIS CASE WON, AND NOW WITH YOUR BROTHER TESTIMONY TOMORROW WILL PUT THE FINISHING TOUCHES ON THE TRAIL I WILL GET HIM EARLY IN THE MORNING, AND GIVE HIM A RUN DOWN OF WHAT TO EXPECT WHEN GOES ON THE STAND SINCE HE IS STILL A MINOR I WOULD NEED THE JUDGE APPROVAL, FOR YOUR BROTHER TO TESTIFY I AM SURE I WILL GET IT SO WE HAVE NO WORRY THERE NOW ANDRA I WILL CALL YOU FIRST TO THE STAND. MY BROTHER HOW DO YOU KNOW MY BROTHER WHERE IS HE YOU FOUND HIM I NEEED TO TALK TO HIM, YES ANDREA HE REACHED OUT TO ME THE OTHER DAY IT WAS GOING TO BE A SURPRISE WHEN HE CAME BACK TO TOWN, AND I TOLD HIM TO WAIT FOR TOMORROW TO SEE YOU WE WANTED THIS DAY TO BE A DAY TO REMEMBER, NOW AFTER YOUR TESTIMONY I WILL CALL YOUR BROTHER TO THE STAND AFTER THAT THE CASE SHOULD COME TO AN END. WILL THEY BE SENDING MY PARENTS TO PRISON YES ANDRA YOUR PARENTS WILL GO TO

PRISON, FOR HOW LONG ONLY THE JUDGE KNOWS OK MR. REYES I WIL SEE YOU TOMORROW I AM GOING TO TALK TO MY BROTHER TOMORROW, WE HAVE A LOT OF CATCHING UP TO DO HAVE A GOOD NIGHT AND I WILL SPEAK TO YOU IN THE MORNING YES GOOD NIGHT MR REYES. SEE YOU IN THE MORNING AS WE STARTED TO GO BACK TO OUR HOUSE ALL ANDEREA COULD DO WAS THINK ABOUT HER BROTHER WHERER HAD HE BBEEN ALL THESE YEARS AND HOW HAD HE BEEN DOING AS I LOOK AT ANDREA, I SEE TEARS COMING OUT OF HER EYES ANDREA WHY ARE YOU CRYING AS ANDREA STANDS THEIR SILENT LOOKING UPON THE STARS, IN THE SKY YOU KNOW RANDY I HONESTLY THOUGHT I WOULD NEVER SEE MY BROTHER AGAIN AND HOW DID HE KNOW TO COME TO THE COURTHOUSE AT THE RIGHT TIME, WHEN I NEEDED SOMEONE BY MY SIDE WHO WAS BEEN THERE WITH ME AND SAW ALL THE ABUSE I WAS EXPERIENCING. THANK YOU JESUS CHRIST FOR ANSWERING MY PRAYERS AND HELPING ME FIND FREEDOM FROM ALL THE PAIN WILL ANDREA I GURSS WE WILL SOON FIND OUT HOW YOUR BROTHER KNOWS ABOUT THIS, AND WHAT ELSE HE KNOWS I DO NOT HAVE NO MEMORIES WILL HAPPY MEMORIES OF US GROWING UP I WAS ALWAYS LEFT IN THE DARK ABOUT EVERYTHING, MY PARENTS TREATED ME LIKE TRASH AND TREATED HIM WITH LOVE BUT NOW ALL OF THAT HAS COME TO AN END I WILL NEVER GET THOSE DAYS BACK. NO ANDREA YOU WILL NOT GET THE PASS BACK SO HAVE A NEW START WITH YOUR BROTHER YES RANDY I CAN NOT WAIT TO SEE HIM TOMORROW, AND TALK TO HIM WE ARE HOME LET'S GO TO BED I AM TIRED YES MY LOVE I AM TIRED AS WELL GOOD NIGHT, AND TOMORROW WHEN YOU SEE HIM YOU AND YOUR BROTHER WILL THEN START A NEW CHAPTER IN YALLS LIFE A NEW START THAT YOU BOTH DESERVE. AND CREATE HAPPY MEMORIES OF YOU AND HIM AS ANDREA LAID DOWN SHE WAS JUST THINKING ABOUT HER BROTHER AS RANDY TURN TO HER, AS HE TELLS HER I KNOW IT IS GOING TO BE AN EMOTIONAL MOMENT FOR THE BOTH OF YALL SO JUST TAKE YOIUR TIME AND SPEND QUALITY TIME WITH HIM, ASK HIM ALL KINDS OF QUESTIONS ESPECIALLY ABOUT THE WHEN HE WAS THERE AT THE HOUSE WITH YOU OK RANDY I WILL IT IS ALMOST MORNING TIME, LET'S GET SOME REST WE HAVE TO BE AT THE COURTHOUSE EARLY I AM SURE MY BROTHER WILL BE ONE OF THE FIRST ONE'S THERE. HE LIKE TO BE EARLY FOR EVERYTHING SO LET US REST AND WE WILL TALK IN THE MORNING AS ANDREA FINALLY FELL ASLEEP SHE COULD NOT FALL INTO A DEEP SLEEP, ALL SHE COULD DO WAS THINK ABOUT HER BROTHER WHOM SHE HAD NOT SEEN IN A FEW YEARS AS THEY WAKE UP WE WILL SEE HOW THE DAY GOES, NOW THAT HER BROTHER IS BACK IN HER LIFE SHE FEEL'S HER LIFE IS ALMOST COMPLETE GOOD MORNING RANDY GOOD MORNING

ANDREA LET'S GET READY WE HAVE TO BE AT THE COURTHOUSE REAL SOON I AM READY, I AM JUST WAITING ON YOU WILL I AM READY AS WELL AS RANDY AND ANDREA HEADS TOWARDS THE COURTHOUSE ANDREA IS QUIET JUST THINKING ABOUT FINALLY BEING ABLE TO MEET HER BROTHER. RANDY HERE WE ARE AT THE COURTHOUSE YES WE ARE AND LOOK OVER THERE WHERE ANDREA RIGHT THERE WITH THE ATTORNEY, I BELIEVE THAT IS YOUR BROTHER ANDREA COULD NOT MOVE MY BROTHER HE IS HERE LET'S GO TALK TO HIM IT WILL BE OK AS ANDREA GOT TO WHERE ANDY WAS THEY JUST STOOD THEIR LOOKING AT EACH OTHER, NOT SAYING A WORD THEY COULD NOT TAKE THEIR EYES OF EACH OTHER THEN AS THEY STARTED CRYING THEY GAVE EACH OTHER A BIG HUG, ANDERA ASK HER BROTHER ANDY WHERE DID YOU GO ANDREA IT HURT ME TO LEAVE YOU IN ALL OF THAT PAIN AND ABUSE I WAS JUST A LITTEL KID, I COULD NOT DO ANYTHING TO HELP YOU AND EVERY TIME THEY DID THINGS TO YOU I WAS SCARED AND I WOULD HIDE UNDER MY BLANKETS. AND CRY OUT FOR SOMEONE TO COME AND HELP YOU ANDY YOU LEFT ME THERE WITH THOSE MONSTERS WHERE DID YOU GO. AFTER I LEFT THE HOUSE I DID NOT KNOW WHAT I WAS GOING TO DO AFTER ALL I WAS JUST A LITTLE KID I WAS WAKING DOWN OUR STREET IN FEAR NOT KNOWING WHERE I WAS GOING, AND I ENDED UP AT MY BEST FRIENDS HOUSE I SAT ON HIS FRONT PORCH IN TEARS WONDERING WHAT I WAS GOING TO DO, AND WHERE WAS I GOING TO STAYED THEN I HEARD THE FRONT DOOR OF THE HOUSE OPEN HIS MOM CAME OUT AND SAID OH NO WHAT IS WRONG COME INSIDE, WHAT HAPPENED I CAN NOT TAKE IT MY PARENTS KEEP ABUSING ANDREA EVERY DAY FOR NO REASON AND I AM SCARED THEY ARE GOING TO ABUSE ME TO. PLEASE LET ME STAY WITH YALL DON'T MAKE ME GO BACK TO THAT HOUSE OF TORTURE OK YOU CAN STAY HERE, SO THAT IS WHERE I BEEN FOR THE PAST FEW YEARS WHY DIDN'T YOU EVER COME BACK FOR ME WHY DID YOU LET ME SUFFER NO ANDREA I COULD NOT DO ANYTHING, BUT I AM HERE NOW I KNOW IT'S LATE BUT I AM HERE FOR YOU NOW, AND I AM SO SORRY I LFET THE WAY I DID IT IS OK MY BELOVED BROTHER THE IMPORTANT THING IS THAT YOU ARE BACK WITH ME AND WE CAN START A NEW LIFE TOGETHER. YOU ARE MY LITTLE BROTHER I LOVE OH YES SISTER I LOVE YOU AND MISS YOU SO MUCH AND WOW I SEE YOU STILL KNOW HOW TO STIR THINGS UP, I HAVE NEVER SEEN ANYONE AS MUCH TROUBLE AS MOM AND DAD ARE SO TELL ME WHAT DID THE ATTORNEY SAY ABOUT HOW MUCH TIME THEY ARE GETTING IN PRISON, HE IS LOKING AT 50 YEARS FOR DAD AND 30 YEARS FOR MOM BUT WE WILL WAIT AND SEE WHAT THE JUDGE DECIDES TO GIVE THEM. ANYWAY IT IS GETTING LATE TIME TO GO INSIDE THE COURTHOUSE NOW THE ATTORNEY IS GOING TO TALK TO YOU AND GO OVER

THE QUESTION HE IS GOING TO ASK YOU, AND AS YOU TAKE THE STAND ANDY I AM LETTTING YOU KNOW THAT YOUR TESTIMONY IS GOING TO BE AS IMPORTAN AS MIND FOR ME AND YOU WERE THE ONLY ONES THERE WHEN ALL THE ABUSE HAPPEN. AND MAKE SURE YOU TELL THE TRUTH WE DO NOT NEED THESES TWO MONSTERS GET OFF AS ANDREA WAS SAYING THIS TO ANDY THE ATTORNEY SAID WE HAVE THIS CASE WON, SO LET US STAND TOGETHER AND FINISH WHAT WE STARTED ALMOST A YEAR AGO WOW ANDREA THIS HAS BEEN GOING ON FOR ALMOST A YEAR YES ANDY IT HAS, AND AGAIN I AM GLAD YOU ARE HERE LIKE I SAID I MISS YOU SO MUCH. SO GO TALK TO THE ATTORNEY AND HE WILL LET YOU KNOW EVERYTHING HE IS GOING TO QUESTION YOU ON, AND I JUST WANT THIS TO BE OVER WITH I AM READY TO PUT THIS CHAPTER IN MY LIFE BEHIND ME AND START A NEW CHAPTER IN MY LIFE, FREE AND HAPPY WITH THE PEOPLE THAT I LOVE AND THAT TRUELY LOVE ME YES SISTER THAT IS WHY I CAME BACK SO I COULD BE WITH YOU, AND WE START OUR LIFE TOGETHER I WANT A HAPPY LIFE WITH MY SISTER YOU WILL WIN THIS AND THEN AFTERWARDS WE WILL GO BACK TO OUR GRANDMA HOUSE AND WE WILL BE HAPPY AND FREE.

CHAPTER 9　　　　　THE FINAL JUDGMENT

YES, BROTHER WE WILL AND I KNOW IT WILL TURN OUT GREAT THE ATTORNEY SAID THAT AFTER TODAY IT MIGHT BE OVER WITH AND WE WILL SEE WHAT IS GOING TO HAPPEN TO OUR PARENTS, AFTER MY TESTIMONY AND YOUR TESTIMONY THAT WILL BE ALL THE COURT NEEEDS TO PUT THE MONSTERS AWAY FOR A GOOD, YES SISTER THIS IS TRUE WILL IT IS GETTING LATE TIME TO GET INSIDE AND I CAN NOT WAIT TO SEE THE SURPRISE LOOK ON OUR PARENTS FACE. WHEN THEY SEE YOU WALK INTO THAT COURTROOM, I AM SURE EVERYONE IS ALREADY IN THERE WAITING FOR US, I AM READY. JUST MAKE SURE YOU AND ANDY ARE READY TO DO WHAT WE NEED TO DO THAT WE MAY HAVE VICTORY. ALL ANDREA COULD DO WAS JUST THINK ABOUT WHAT WAS

GOING TO HAPPEN WHICH WILL BE THE MOST IMPORTANT PART OF TEH TRAIL AS TEH WHOLE WORLD LOOKS ON IN THE COURTROOM ANDREA BROTHER IS SITTING THER AS HE SPEAKS HURTFUL WORDS I CN NOT BELIEVE I STOOD BACK AND LET MY PARENTS CAUSE ALL THAT PAIN AND SUFFERING TO MY SISTER ANDREA SHE DID NOT DESERVE THS SHE IS A GOOD PERSON WITH A BEAUTIFUL HEART AND I WILL MAKE SURE THEY GET WHAT THEY HAVE COING TO THEM ONLY IF I WAS A LITTLE OLDERE BACK THEN I COULD HAVE HELPED HER I PRAY SHE FORGIVES ME AS ANDY SIT HERE IN TEARS ANDREA GOES TO HIM ANDY I FORGIVE YOIU IT WAS NOT YOIUR FAULT YOU WERE JUST A YOUND BOY YOU WERE SCARED AND DID NOT KNOW WHAT TO DO THE PASS IS OVER WITH NOW WE MUCH FOCUS ON TEH FUTURE AND GETTING TO KNOW EACH OTHER AGAIN I FORGOT TO TELL YOU WHEN WE ARE DONE HER WITH THE COURT AND RANDY IS DONE WITH HIS COURT CASE THEN WE ARE GOING TO GO STAY WITH OUR AUNT AND GRANDMA YOU HAVE NOT MET THEMI I TELL YOU BROTHER THEY ARE WONDERFUL PEOPLE FULL OF LOVE AND HAPPINESS WOULD OU LIKE TO COME AND LIVE WITH US TH RE WITH THEEM YES T AT WILL BE GREAT OK ANDREA LET'S GO TALK TO THE ATTORNEY AND SEE WHATS GOING TO HAPPEN FOR THIS IS IMPORTANT HELLO MR. REYES HELLO ANDREA AND ANDY AS THEY WERE TALKING RANDY GOT A PHONE CALL HIS NAME CAME OUT ON THE LOUD SPEAKER THAT HE HAD A PHONE CALL WAITING FOR HIM IN THE LOBBY, ANDREA I WILL BE RIGHT BACK I HAVE A CALL WAITING I DO NOT KNOW WHO COULD BE CALLING ME HERE AT THE COURTHOUSE, AS RANDY WALKS DOWN THE HALL WONDERING WHO WOULD BE CALLING HIM HE GET'S TO THE DESK GRAB THE PHONE AT FIRST NOT SAYING A WORD THEN SPEAKS IN A LOW VOICE HELLO THIS IS RANDY HOW CAN I HELP YOU. RANDY HOW YOU DOING THIS IS DETECTIVE SMITH I JUST CALLED TO INFORM YOU THAT YOUR TRIAL WILL BE IN TWO WEEKS JUST MAKE SURE YOU ARE PREPARED, AND I NEED YOUR GIRLFRIEND ANDERA THERE WITH YOU I WILL BE THERE HAVE TO GO I AM IN COURT RIGHT NOW WITH ANDREA. THIS SHOULD BE THE LAST DAY IN COURT AS RANDY HANGS UP THE PHONE HIS HAND STAY'S ON THE RECIVER AND HE STARTED TO THINK ABOUT THE UP COMING DAY'S WHEN HE WILL HAVE TO GO TO COURT, THEN HE SAY'S IT STARTING ALL OVER AGAIN AS HE STARTS WALKING DOWN THE HALL AND GOES TO TALK TO ANDREA ABOUT THE PHONE CALL THE ATTORNEY INSTRUCTS THEM TO GO INSIDE, ANDREA LOOKS ON IN THE COURTROOM LOOK RANDY MY CASE I JUST STARTING I HOPE THAT ALL OF THIS WILL BE OVER. ANDREA I AM HERE BY YOUR SIDE AS ANDY TALKS TO THE ATTORNEY ONCE AGAIN BEFORE THEY GO INTO THE COURTROOM ANDREA TELLS RANDY YOU KNOW YOU SAVED MY LIFE, I WIIILL ALWAYS LOVE YOU AND

LIKE THE WIND I KNOW THAT YOU WILL ALWAYS BE THERE FOR ME AND WITH ME YES ANDREA YOU ARE MY EVERYTHING I AM BELSSED TO HAVE YOU, AS WE WALK TO GRAB OUR SEATS I SEE MY PARENTS SITTING THEIR AND FOR THE FIRST TIME I SEE THEM IN TEARS AS I SMILE AND WALK AWAY, THEY LOOK AT ME AND SAID TO ME WE ARE SORRY FOR ALL THE PAIN AND ABUSE WE PUT YOU THREW I JUST LOOK AT THEM AND SMILED AND DID NOT SAY A WORD, THEN WHEN THEY SAW ANDY WALK IN MY MOM STARTED CRYING OUT LOUD AND SAID MY SON YOU ARE HERE TO HELP DEFEND YOUR MOM AND DAD, HE SMILE AND SAID NO MOM I AM HERE FOR ANDREA ALL THE PAIN YOU BOTH CAUSE HER FOR NO REASON WAS NOT RIGHT AND NOW YOU BOTH WILL PAY FOR TH PAIN YALL CAUSED ANDREA, AND THE OTHER KIDS AFTER ANDY SAID THIS HE WENT TO SIT DOWN BEHIND ANDREA AS THE JUDGE WALKS IN ALL RISE COURT IN SESSSION THE HONORABLE JUDGE WRIGHT PRESIDING ALL MAY BE SEATED, GOOD MORNING COURT GOOD MORNING JUDGE MR. REYES IS YOUR WITNESS READY YES YOUR HONOR CALL YOUR FIRST WITNESS. I CALL ANDREA BACK TO THE STAND AS ANDREA WALKS BACK TO THE STAND HER PARENTS ATTORNEY SAID OBJECTION YOUR HONOR, THIS WITNESS ALREADY HAD THEIR TIME ON THE STAND I SEE NO NEED FOR THIS WITNESS TO BE CALLED AGAIN OVRERULE ANDREA YOU MAY TAKE THE STAND, AND REMEMBER YOU ARE STILL UNDER OATH YES YOUR HONOR ANDREA I HAVE IN MY HAND A SECOND LETTER YOU WROTE TO ROBERT CAN YOU PLEASE REAID IT TO THE COURT AND EXPLAIN THE EXPERIENCE THAT YOU WENT THROUGH. THE DAY IN QUESTION THIS LETTER IS DATED JULY 23 1978 HELLO ROBERT I AM HERE IN MY ROOM IN PAIN TRYING TO STOP THE BELEEDNG IT HURTS SO MUCH TO WALK, MY DAD OVER DID IT THIS TIME I GOT HOME A LITTLE LATE FROM SCHOOL AND MY MOM SLAPPED ME WHEN I WALKED IN AND SAID YOUR WORTHLESS AND YOU ARE LATE GO TO YOUR ROOM AND GET READY FOR WHAT YOU HAVE COMING TO YOU, AS I WAS WALKING TO MY ROOM I SAW MY DAD AND HIS TWO FRIENDS LOOKING AT ME FROM HEAD TO TOE LICKING THEIR LIPS I GOT SCARE .I WENT IN MY ROOM AND I STARTED CRYING THEN THEY CAME IN ONE AT A TIME AS ANDREA WAS READING THE LETTER TEARS WERE FALLING FROM HER EYES, AS SHE CONTINUE ROBERT THEY HURT ME I BEGGED THEM TO STOP AND THEY ALL JUST LAUGHE AT ME THE WORST PART WAS WHEN THEY FINISHED MY DAD CAME IN, AND DID THE SAME THING TO ME AND MY MOM JUST LAUGH. SAYING THAT IS WHAT YOU GET NOW WE HAVE ENOUGH MONEY TO BUY OUR DRUGS AND ALCOHOL IF I DO NOT SHOW UP TO SCHOOL TOMORROW THEN I KILLED MYSELF, I CAN NOT TAKE THIS ANYMORE PLEASE SOMEONE HELP ME GET ME OUT OF THIS TORTURE HELP ME LORD AS ANDREA FINISH READING THE LETTER SHE DROP HER HEAD AND

WAS IN TEARS. COULD BEARLY TALK IS THAT THE END ANDREA YES IT IS HOW YOU FEEL AND WHAT WAS GOING THREW YOUR MIND WHEN ALL OF THIS WAS GOING ON I FELT LIKE IF IT WAS MY FAULT, AND I WAS THINKING ABOUT HOW COULD MY PARENTS ALLOW THIS TO HAPPEN TO ME AND HOW COULD MY DAD DO THIS TO ME, I NEVER THOUGHT A DAD COULD DO THIS TO HIS DAUGHTER BUT IT HAPPENED TO ME I PRAY THAT THIS KIND OF ABUSE NEVER HAPPENS TO ANOTHE GIRL, I HAVE NO MORE QUSTIONS MR. SANCHEZ WOULD YOU LIKE TO CROSS EXAMINE YES YOUR HONOR I WOULD, ANDREA HOW ARE YOU FEELING I AM OK I JUST WANT THIS TO BE OVER YES I KNOW YOU DO SO LET ME ASK YOU HOW DID YOU DRESS IN FRONT OF YOUR DAD, OBJECTION YOUR HONOR HER WARDROBE IS NOT ON TRIAL HERE YOUR HONOR THE WAY SHE DRESSED COULD OF TRIGGER HOW HER DAD LOOKED AT HER, SUSTAIN CHANGE THE QUESTION MR. SANCHEZ YES YOUR HONOR DID YOU EVER GIVE YOUR DAD ANY REASON TO DO THIS TO YOU, NO I DID NOT THEY ARE JUST MONSTERS THAT NEED TO BE PUT AWAY NO FURTHRE QUESTIONS YOU CAN STEP DOWN ANDREA MR REYES CALL YOUR NEXT WITNESS, I CALL ANDY GARCIA TO THE STAND AND DO YOU SWEAR TO TELL THE TRUTH THE WHOLE TRUTH AND NOTHING BUT THE TRUTH SO HELP YOU GOD, I DO YOU MAY BE SEATED ANDY CAN YOU TELL THE COURT IN YOUR OWN WORDS WHAT HAPPENED TO YOUR SISTER ANDREA AND WHAT YOU HEARD OR SAW WILL, THAT NIGHT I HEARD HER CRY AND SCREAM I GOT SCARE SO I WENT TO HER ROOM TO SEE WHAT HAD HAPPENDE AND I SAW MY DAD WALKING OUT OF HER ROOOM, ZIPPING UP HIS PANTS I LOOKED ANDREA ON THE BED HOLDING HER STOMACH AND THE BED WAS FULL OF BLOOD, I WAS SCARED WHEN I SAW THAT I WENT TO TELL MY MOM WHAT I SAW AND SHE JUST LOOKED AT ME AND SAID IS ANDREA DEAD I SAID NO BUT SHE IS BLEEDING ALOT, GET OUT OF MY ROOM I AM NOT WORRIED ABOUT HER NOW GO BACK TO BED AND LEAVE ME ALONE AFTER I WENT BACK TO ANDREA ROOM, I TRIED TO HELP HER AS MUCH AS I COULD HOW OLD WERE YOU I WAS ONLY 7 YEARS OLD AND ANDREA WAS ONLY 10 YEARS OLD AND WHEN SHE TURNED 11 YEARS OLD THINGS GOT WORSE, HOW DID THEY GET WORST ANDY TELL ME WHAT MADE IT WORSE MY PARENTS STARTED DRINKING MORE AND MORE AND DOING MORE DRUGS THAN BEFORE. THEY HAD ALL KINDS OF MAN COME OVER TO THE HOUSE AND GO INTO ANDREA ROOM I COULD NOT TAKE IT ANYMORE EVERY DAY WAS A DIFFERENT MAN, ONE DAY I TRIED TO STOP THEM BUT MY DAD SLAPPED ME AND SAID DON'T YOU DARE INTERFERE WITE OUR MONEY NOW GO TO YOUR ROOM AND DO NOT COME OUT UNTIL WE TELL YOU TO. I SAT IN MY ROOM AND I COULD JUST HEAR MY SISTER CRY AND PLEAD FOR THEM TO STOP BUT THEY NEVER DID THANK YOU

ANDY I HAVE NO FURTHER QUESTIONS. MR. SANCHEZ WOULD YOU LIKE TO CROSS EXAMINE YES YOU HONOR WILL ANDY THAT IS A GOOD STORY HOW OLD DID YOIU SAY WERE WHEN THIS WAS HAPPENING, I SAID I WAS 7 YEARS OLD HOW CAN YOU REMEMBER SOMTHING LIKE THAT WHEN YOU WERE ONLY 7 YEARS OLD, ARE YOU SURE YOU ARE NOT MAKING THIS UP TO GET BACK AT YOUR PARENTS FOR SOMETHING ELSE. MR. SANCHEZ LET ME ASK YOU A QUESTION DO YOU REMEMBER YOUR CHILDDHOOD OBJECTION YOUR HONOR, I DO NOT SEE WHAT MY CHILDHOOD HAS TO DO WITH THIS CASE OVERRULE ANSWER THE QUESTION YES I REMEMBER MY CHILDHOOD HOW FAR BACK DO YOU REMEMBER I REMEMBER BACK TO WHEN I WAS 7 YEARS OLD, SO HOW IS IT FAIR TO SAY THAT YOU CAN REMEMBER YOUR CHILDHOOD BUT I CAN NOT REMEMBER WHAT HAPPEN IN MINE AND YOU SAY THIS IS A PAY BACK. YES IT IS THEY MUST PAY FOR WHAT THEY DID TO MY SISTER YOU CAN NOT STAND THERE AND SAY THEY ARE NO GUILTY YOU WAS NOT THERE WHEN THIS WAS HAPPENING, YOU DID NOT WITNESS THESE MEN ALL OVER MY SISTER YOU DID NOT GO UNDER YOUR COVERS AS YOU HEARD HER YELLED AND SCREAM AND BEG THEM TO STOP, SO DON'T SAY THEY ARE NOT GUILTY NO MORE QUESTIONS YOU CAN STEP DOWN ANDY AS HE WENT TO HIS SEAT THE JUDGE SPOKE ANY MORE WITNESS MR.REYES NO YOUR HONOR THE PLANTIFF REST,MR SANCHEZ NO YOUR HONOR THE DEFENSE REST MR. REYES WOULD YOU LIKE TO PRESENT YOUR CLOSING ARGUMENT YES YOUR HONOR LADIES AND GENTLEMEN OF THE JURY, AS THE TRIAL WENT ON ALL THESE MONTH YOU ALL HAVE WITNESSED HOW THESE TO PEOPLE DESTROYED THE LIFES OF MANY PEPLE INCLUDING THE LIFE OF ANDREA THERE DAUGHTER A DAUGHTER THEY WERE SUPPOSED TO LOVE AND PROTECT, BUT THEY DID NOT THEY SPENT HOURS AND DAYS TORTURING HER AND ABUSING HER AND CHILD TRAFFICKING IMAGINE THIS BEING YOUR DAUGHTER. THEY EVEN HAD THE NERVE TO KIDNAP ANOTHER CHILD TO CONTINUE THEIR DRUG USE I ASK THE JURY TO COME BACK WITH THE VERDICT OF GUILTY, FOR CHILD ABUSE CHILD TRAFFICKING AND ASSAULT CAUSING BODILY INJURY AND FOR THE MOM THE VERDICT OF ACCESSORY TO ALL THE CHARGES THE COURT PRESENTED THANK YOU. MR. SANCHEZ WOULD YOU LIKE TO PRESENT YOUR CLOSING ARGUMENT NO YOUR HONOR WILL JURORS YOU MAY LEAVE THE COURTROOM AND THANK YOU FOR YOUR SERVICES. AS THE JURORS WENT TO THE JURY ROOM TO BEGIN THEIR DELIBERATIONS EVERYONE WAS ON THEIR TOES HOPING FOR A GOOD VERDICT LET US GO ANDREA, NO I AM GOING TO WAIT HERE IN THE COURTROOM UNTIL THE JURY RETURNS I WILL WAIT HERE WITH YOU THIS IS FINALLY THE MOMENT YOU HAVE BEEN WAITING FOR ALL OF YOUR LIFE, YES RANDY YOU DO NOT

KNOW HOW LONG I WAITED FOR THIS DAY TO HAPPEN I EVEN HAD DREAMS ABOUT THE DAY I WOULD GET MY PAY BACK ON MY PARENTS,NOW WE ARE MOMENTS AWAY FROM SEEING MY VICTORY YES ANDREA AND WHEN THOSE DOORS OPEN YOU WILL SEE YOUR HAPPINESS THE JURY DID NOT TAKE LONG THEY WERE BACK IN THE COURTROOM WITHIN 1 HOUR, AS ANDREA TAKE'S HER SEAT SHE SEE THE JURY WALK BACK INTO THE COURTROOM HER HEART JUST DROP WAITING TO HEAR THE VERDICT THE WHOLE COURTROOM WAS SILENT ON THE EDGE OF THERE SEAT, AS THE JURORS GRAB THERE SEAT THE JUDGE ASK DID THE JURORS REACH A VERDICT YES WE HAVE YOUR HONOR, PLEASE READ THE OUTCOME ON THE CHARGE OF CHILD ABUSE WE FIND THE DEFENDANTS GUILTY ON THE CHARGE OF CHILD ENDANGERMENT WE FIND THE DEFENDANTS GUILTY,ON THE CHARGE OF CHILD TRAFFICKING WE FIND THE DEFENDANTS GUILTY THANK YOU LADIES AND GENTLMENT OF THE JURY YOU ALL ARE DISMISSED. AS ANDREA HEARD THE VERDICT OF GUILTY ON ALL THE CHARGES SHE DROP TO HER KNEES AND CRYED AND CRYED THANKING GOD FOR ANSWERING HER PRAYERS, WILL THE DEFENDANTS STAND FOR SENTENCING MR GARCIA I AM SHOCKED AT HOW YOU WERE WITH YOUR DAUGHTER, ALL MY YEARS AS A JUDGE I NEVER HEARD OF A CASE MORE DISTURBING I HOPE YOU REALIZE ONE DAY THAT WHAT YOU DID WAS NOT NORMAL, MAY GOD HELP YOU MR GARCIA RISE FOR SENTENCING I SENTENCE YOU LIFE TO PRISON WITHOUT THE POSSIBILITY OF PAROLE WHEN THE JUDGE GAVE ANDREA DAD THIS SENTENCE SHE DROPPED TO HER KNEES AND CRIED, HAPPY TEARS WE DID IT HE IS GONE FOR GOOD YES MY LOVE LET'S SEE WHAT YOUR MOM IS GOING TO GET MRS. GARCIA I AM HEART BROKEN THAT YOIU ALLOW THIS TO HAPPEN TO YOUR CHILD AND OTHER CHILDREN. FOR YOUR UNIMAGINABLE INVOLVEMENT I SENTENCE YOU TO 40 YEARS IN PRISON WITHOUT THE POSSIBILITY OF PAROLE AS ANDREA SEE HER PARENTS TAKEN AWAY SHE IS IN MUCH TEARS BUT HAPPY TEARS, AND SHE TELLS HER PARENTS WELCOME TO YOUR HELL IN PRISON NOW IT IS TIME FOR YOU TO EXPERIENCE YOUR PAIN AND SUFFERING AND NO ONE THERE TO HELP, THE BALIFF TAKES THE PRISONERS AWAY THE COURT ADJOURNS EVEREYONE STANDS AS THE JUDGE LEAVES. AS THE JUDGE LEAVES THE COURTROOM ANDREA EYES ARE FILLED WITH TEARS OF HAPPINESS AS SHE TELLS RANDY WILL IT IS FINALLY OVER ,THEY WILL NEVER HURT ANOTHER KID YES MY LOVE THEY ARE GONE FOR GOOD AS ANDREA AND RANDY REJOICE OVER THE FINAL VERDICT JUDY'S DAD STILL HAD A LOT OF ANGER THE ONLY THOUGHT GOING THREW HIS HEAD WAS HAVING ANDRE DAD KILLED. AND HE SWORE NOT TO REST UNTIL HE IS DEAD NO ONE KNOWS WHAT HE HAS PLANNED WILL RANDY LET'S GO HOME AND

CELEBATE OUR VICTORY, AS THEY GOT TO THERE HOUSE THE DETECTIVE WAS THERE WAITING FOR RANDY HELLO DETECTIVE HOW MAY I HELP YOU WILL RANDY I CAME TO INFORM YOU THAT YOU WILL NOT NEED TO GO TO COURT NEXT WEEK, WHY DON'T TELL ME THEY RELEASE JOEY WILL JOEY IS GONE BUT NOT BECAUSE HE WAS RELEASED THEN WHAT HAPPNED THE OTHER NIGHT THERE WAS A RIOT IN THE JAIL, AND JOEY WAS ENGAGED IN THE RIOT HE GOT STABBED 21 TIME'S IN THE CHEST HE DID NOT MAKE IT TO THE HOSPITAL AS THE DETECTIVE SAID THIS BOTH ANDREA AND RANDY WERE SHOCKED THEY HAD NO WORDS TO SAY. AS THE DETECTIVE WAS LEAVING RANDY SAID THANK YOU RANDY LOOKED AT ANDREA AND SAID I AM SORRY HE IS DEAD WHY ARE YOU SORRY HE TRIED TO KILL YOU, YES I KNOW BUT TWO WRONGS DO NOT MAKE IT RIGHT I WANTED JUSTICE THE RIGHT WAY NOT LIKE THS MAY GOD FORGIVE HIM FOR ALL HE HAS DONE WRONG. AS RANDY AND ANDREA WERE TALKING ABOUT THIS JUDY DAD WAS TRYING TO FIND OUT WHICH PRISON ANDREA DAD WAS GOING TO BE IN HE WAITED PATIENTLY UNTILL HE WAS ABLE TO GET THE INFORMATION HE NEEDED TO HAVE HIM KILLED, ON THE INSIDE OF THOSE PRISON WALLS WHAT THEY DID NOT KNOW MR. TORRES HAD LOTS OF CONNECTIONS ON THE INSIDE SO HE WILL BE SEEKING JUSTICE IN HIS OWN WAY, BACK AT ANDREA HOUSE ANDREA WAS LOOKING AT RANDY AS THEY BOTH SAT THERE NOT SAYING A WORD JUST THINKING ABOUT WHAT THEY FOUND OUT, AND AS THEY LOOKED AT EACH OTHER RANDY SAID TO ANDREA WILL MY LOVE IT LOOK LIKE I WILL NOT HAVE TO GO TO COURT AFTER ALL NOW WHAT IS OUR NEXT MOVE, WHAT DO WE DO NOW ANDRA STAYED QUITE THEN SHE LOOKED AT RANDY WITH A BIG SMILE WILL RANDY I ACCOMPLISHED WHAT I WAS SEEEKING THERE IS ONLY ONE THING LEFT TO DO AND THAT IS TO MOVE BACK TO MY AUNT AND GRANDMA SUSIE HOUSE, THEN WHEN WE THERE REGISTER TO GO BACK TO SCHOOL I HAVE ONE YEAR LEFT I MUST FINISH SCHOOL AND THEN ENROLL IN COLLAGE YES YOU ARE RIGHT, I NEED TO FINISH SCHOOL TOO LET'S TELL ANDY WHAT OUR PLANS ARE ANDY COME HERE WE NEED TO TALK TO YOU WHAT IS IT WE ARE DONE HERE AND WE ARE MOVING BACK TO GRANDMA HOUSE, ARE YOU COMING WITH US YES ANDREA I WILL BE GOING BCK WITH YALL AS THEY WERE MAKING THEIR FUTURE PLANS THE PHONE RANG, ANDREA ANSWERE THE PHONE HELLO WHO IS SPEAKING HELLO IT IS JUDY DAD HOW ARE YOIU DOING MR. TORRES IS THERE SOMETHING THAT YOU NEED YES I WOULD LIKE TO KNOW WHAT PRISON YOUR DAD IS IN, HMMM WHY WOULD YOU LIKE TO KNOW THAT WHAT ARE YOUR PLANS NO PLANS I AM JUST MAKING SUREK HE IS NOT ABLE TO ESCAPE AND HURT ANYONE ELSE OK HE IS IN RAMSEY 3 NEAR HOUSTON TX. OK ANDREA THANKS A LOT. YES SIR AS

THEY HUNG UP THE PHONE ANDREA STAYED SILENT, AS SHE WALKED BACK INTO THE ROOM WHO WAS ON THE PHONE THAT WAS A STRANGE CALL WHO WAS IT RANDY IT WAS JUDY DAD WHAT DID HE WANT, HE WANTED INFORMATION ON WHAT PRISON MY DAD WAS AT AND DID YOU TELL HIM YES I DID DO YOU THINK HE WILLL TRY TO GET HIM KILLED, HE WAS MAD AT THE COURTHOUSE BUT WE WILL WAIT AND SEE WHAT HAPPENS YOU NKOW RANDY IT HAS BEEN A YEAR SINCE I LEFT GRANDMA HOUSE, RANDY STAYED QUIET AND DID NOT SAY A WORD THEN HE SAID ANDREA I HAVE TO TELL YOU SOMETHING WHAT IS IT RANDY, WHEN I WAS YOUNGER I TRIED A NEW DRUG THAT CAME TO TOWN AND IT WAS THE BEST THING THAT HAS HAPPPNED I LOVED IT MORE THAN MY OWN LIFE. YES, EVERYONE WAS DOING IT SO I DECIDED TO TRY IT THE NAME OF THE DRUG WAS CRACK COCAINE, AND AFTERE THE FIRST HIT I GOT HOOKED I STAYED ON THAT DRUG FOR 6 MONTHS I HATED IT BUT COULD NOT LEAVE THE DRUG ALONE NO MATTER HOW I TRIED I LOST EVERYTHING. WHAT DID YOU LOSE I LOST EVERYONE RESPECT I LOST THEIR TRUST AND NO ONE TRUSTE ME IN THEIR HOUSE EVERY TIME THEY SAW ME COMING, THEY WOULD SAY HERE COMES RANDY HIDE YOUR STUFF HE LIKES TO STEAL FOR HIS DRUGS BUT MOST OF ALL I LOST MY SELF RESPECT, I COULD NOT BELIEVE WHAT I WAS DOING TO MY FAMILY I WOULD STEAL FROM THEM JUST GET A 10 DOLLAR ROCK WHICH THE HIGH WOULD ONLY LAST 10 MINUTES, I WAS THROWING MY LIFE AWAY AND DID NOT CARE ALL I CARED ABOUT WAS WHERE MY NEXT HIGH WAS COMING FROM. I ALMOST OVER DOSED 3 TIMES BUT THAT DID NOT STOP ME SO RANDY HOW DID YOU STOP DOING THOSE DRUGS IT HAPPEN ON THE SADDEST DAY OF MY LIFE, WHAT HAPPEN MY GRANDMA PASSED AWAY AS I WAS AT HER FUNERAL I SAT THERE IN TEARS THINKING ABOUT ALL THE PAIN AND SUFFERING I CAUSED MY FAMILY, A FAMILY THAT LOVED ME I TURNED MY BACK ON THEM AND WENT THE OTHER WAY IN THE DEADLY WORLD OF DRUGS SO THAT DAY I MADE A PROMISE AT MY GRANDMA FUNERAL, I PROMISE I WOULD NEVER DO DRUGS AGAIN AND SINCE THAT DAY I STOPPED ANDREA IT TOOK ME A LONG TIME TO GET EVERYONE TRUST AND RESPECT BACK, BUT SLOWLY I GOT EVERYONE TO TRUST ME AND RESPEFCT ME AGAIN I AM HER TO TELL YOU THE WORLD OF DRUGS IS NO GOOD IT WILL KILL YOU TEAR YOU DOWN, AND HURT THE PEOPLE THAT LOVE YOU AND CARE FOR YOU I AM BLESSED I LEFT THE DRUGS WHEN I DID I LOVE YOU RANDY AND THANK YOU FOR TELLING ME THIS. I LOVE YOU TOO AS RANDY AND ANDREA WERE THERE TALKING IT WAS DIFFERENT FOR HER DAD AS HE SAT IN HIS PRISON CELL, HE GOT A VISIT FROM ANOTHER INMATE SO YOU ARE ANDREA GARCIA DAD THE FATHER OF THAT POOR DEFENSELESS LITTLE GIRL, THAT COULD NOT PROTECT HER SELF YOU

TORTURE AND ABUSE AND RAPE HER DUDE SHE WAS YOUR DAUGHTER AND ONLY 12 YEARS OLD I SHOULD KILL YOU RIGHT NOW, BUT I AM NOT WE ARE GOING TO MAKE YOU SUFFER THE WAY YOU AND THOSE MAN MADE ANDREA AND JUDY SUFFER, JUDY TORRES WAS ONLY A 12 YEAR OLD GIRL SHE WAS ENJOYING HER DAY AT THE PARK UNTIL YOU INTERFERE WITH HER LIFE AND MADE HER LIFE A LIVING HELL. SO I SAY TO YOU WELCOME TO YOUR HELL EVERYDAY THAT YOU ARE HERE WE ARE GOING TO MAKE YOUR LIFE A LIVING HELL FROM THIS DAY FORWARD EVERY ONE IN THIS BLOCK CELL IS YOUR DADDY, AS THE INMATE WAS LEAVING HIS CELL HE GRABBED HIM BY HIS THROAT AND SAID ONCE AGAIN WELCOME TO HELL THE FOLLOWING MORNING THE TORTURE STARTED TWO INMATES WENT INTO MR. GARCIA CELL AND SAID TO HIM LET'S SEE HOW GOOD YOU ARE. MAKE DADDY HAPPY HE TRIED TO FIGHT THEM OFF BUT THEY OVER POWERED HIM THEY TOOK TURNS ON HIM AND TEARS STARTED COMING OUT OF HIS EYES, HE BEGGED THEM TO STOP THEY JUST LAUGHED AT HIM AND SAID REMEMBERE MAKE YOUR DADDY HAPPY WHEN THEY SAID THAT HE WAS REMINDED OF WHAT HE WOULD TELL ANDREA AND JUDY, THIS WENT ON FOR ABOUT A WEEK HE WOULD GET TORTURE 6 TIMES A DAY AS THE WEEK CAME TO AN END THE FIRST INMATE CAME INTO THE CELL AND SAID THIS IS YOUR LAST DAY WITH US. IT IS TIME FOR YOU TO LEAVE WHERE AM I GOINNG YOU ARE GOING TO HELL THIS IS FROM JUDY DAD AND HE STARTED STABBING HIM TO DEATH, AFTER HE STABBED ANDERA DAD HE STOOD OVER THE BODY AND JUST LOOKED AT HIS DEAD BODY LAYING ON THE PRISON FLOOR, I CAN NOT BELIEVE YOU DID THIS TO YOUR DAUGHTER I ALWAYS WANTED KIDS BUT WAS NOT BLESSED TO HAVE ANY AND YOU WERE BLESSED TO HAVE KIDS, AND INSTEAD OF LOVING YOUR DAUGHTER YOU HURT HER AND HURT MANY MORE KIDS NOW YOU WILL SUFFER FOR ENTERNITY, AFTER HE SAID THIS HE WAS WALKING OUT OF THE CELL AT THAT POINT HE SAW THE PRISON GUARD WAS WALKING TOWRDS HIM AND LOOK INTO THE CELL AND SAW ANDREA DAD LAYING THERE, AND THE OTHER INMATE FULL OF BLOOD ON HIS HANDS AND SHIRT AND ALL OVER THE CELL FLOOR AS THE INMATE STANDS OVER ANDREA DAD HE STILL CAN NOT BELIEVE THAT SOMEONE WAS SO HATEFUL. AND HAD SO MUCH OF A BLACK HEART THAT THEY WOULD HURT THEIR OWN DAUGHTER BUT HE WILL NEVER HURT NO ONE AGAIN HIS LIFE IS OVER, NOW HE WILL PAY THE PRICE FOR ALL THE PAIN AND SUFFERIING HE HAS CAUSE SO MANY PEOPLE AND THERE IS NO ONE TO HELP HIM HE IS GONE FOR GOOD, AT THIS POINT AS HE STANDS THEIR HE TURNS AND LOOKS AT ALL THE BLOOD ALL OVER THE CELL AND AS HE THINKS ABOUT ALL THE KIDS ANDREA DAD HAS HURT AND DESTROYED THIER LIVES, HE IS GLAD OF WHAT HE DID HE

KNOWS IT WAS WRONG IN GOD'S EYES TO KILL HIM BUT HE ALSO NEW THAT THIS PERSON WAS FULL OF HATRED AND EVIL, AND HE NEEDED TO BE PUT OUT OF THIS WORLD SO AS HE LOOKS OUT THE WINDOW AND AS HE STIRS DOWN AS IF HE COULD NOT BELIEVE WHAT HAD JUST HAPPNE, WITH THE BLOOD ON HIS HANDS HE TURN AND LOOKS AROUND FOR A BIT HE FEELS LOST AND DID NOT KNOW WHAT WAS GOING TO HAPPPEN NEXT, HE NEW THAT WHEN THE GURARD FINDS OUT HE KILLED ANOTHER INMATE HE WOULD NEVER GET OUT SO HE IS STANDING OVER ANDREA DAD STILL HOLDING THE KNIFE IN HIS HAND, AND AS HE LOOKS UP HE SEE THE GUARD AND THE GUARD SEE HIM STANDING OVER ANDREA DAD DEAD BODY, HE SAY'S IN A LOW VOICE YOU ARE FULL OF EVIL AND I HATE YOU THE CHANCE YOU HAD TO BE A GOOD DAD TO YOUR DAUGHTER, YOU THROUGH IT TO ONE SIDE SHE IS A GIFT,BUT NOW HER LIFE IS OVER AND DESTROYED NOW YOU WILL WITNESS AND FEEL WHAT IT IS TO ASK FOR HELP AND NO ONE AROUND TO HELP YOU. FOR YOU WILL BE LIVING YOUR LIFE IN HELL AS HE FINISH SPEAKING THE INMATE TURNS AND SAYS TO THE GUARD I COULD NOT HOLD BACK ANYMORE SO YES I KILLED HIM, NOW WHAT WILL HAPPENTO ME THE GUARD LOOKS AND ASK HIM WHAT ARE YOU TAKING ABOUT I DO NOT SEE NOTHING HERE, THE INMATE JUST SMILED AND WENT BACK TO HIS CELL AS HE THOUGHT THIS MAN MADE ANDREA SUFFER NOW HE WILL SUFFER WHERE EVER HE GOES I JUST HOPE THAT POOR GIRL IS DOING GOOD NOW, I KNOW SHE HAS BEEN THREW A LOT THE INMATE IS FULLY SURPRISE OF EVERYTHING THAT HAS JUST HAPPEN, NOW LET'S SEE WHAT IS HAPPENING BACK AT ANDREA HOUSE THEY SAT THERE THEY WERE JUST THINKING ABOUT WHAT HAPPENED TO JOEY, THIS WAS THE FIRST TIME NO ONE SAID A WORD DURNING DINNER THEY JUST SAT THERE AND FINISHED THEIR DINNER, WHEN THEY WERE DONE THEY HEARD A KNOCK ON THE DOOR HELLO DETECTIVE WHY ARE YOU HERE WHAT HAPPENED NOW AS ANDREA LOOKED AT THE DETECTIVE SHE KNEW SOMETHING WAS WRONG, THE DETECTIVE SAID TO ANDREA LOOKED I AM SORRY TO HAVE TO BE THE ONE TO TELL YOU THIS BUT YOUR DAD GOT KILLED EARLY THIS MORNING, HE WAS STABBED TO DEATH ANDREA SMILED AND SAID OK THATS GREAT ANTHING ELSE I CAN HELP YOU WITH SHE DID NOT CARE SHE KNEW WHO SENT THE HIT, ON HER DAD BUT DID NOT SAY A WORD WOW MY LOVE JUDY DADDY DID IT AND HAD HIM KILLED YES HE DID WILL LET'S TELL ANDY. HEY ANDY COME IN HERE WE NEED TO TELL YOU SOMETHING YES WHAT IS IT ANDREA, WE JUST FOUND OUT THAT OUR DAD GOT STABBED TO DEATH THIS MORNING OK THAT MAKES ONE LESS MONSTER IN THIS WORLD, YES ANDY YOU ARE SO RIGHT WILL CAN NOT WAIT TO TAKE OFF

TOMORROW AND GO HOME YES ANDREA WE ARE ALL READY TO GET OUT OF THIS TOWN AND GO HOME.

THE END

AS ANDREA, RANDY, AND ANDY GET READY FOR THEIR TRIP BACK TO GRANDMA HOUSE THEY ARE ALL HAPPY LITTLE DOES ANDREA KNOWS SHE WILL FIND OUT THE SHOCKING TRUTH THAT SHE HAS A REAL FATHER THAT ABANDON HER WHEN SHE WAS STILL A BABY WILL SHE FORGIVE HER DAD OR WILL SHE TURN HER BACK ON HIM AS HE DID TO HER FIND OUT ALONG WITH MORE SHOCKING DISCOVERY IN THE NEXT BOOK WHICH WILL BE AVAILABLE LATER THIS YEAR

THIS BOOK WAS WRITTEN AND CREATED

BY RANDY FLORES

EMAIL FLORESRANDY003@GMAIL.COM

COPYRIGHT ON 06/09/2024

REGISTERED BY THE STATE OF TEXAS ON 06/09/2024

Made in the USA
Columbia, SC
21 June 2024